DEFENDING SOCRATES

Alex Priou traces modernity's descent into nihilism to its rejection of Socratic philosophizing as unscientific in form and content, and in particular to its assumption that the truth must be sought in abstraction from the good. *Defending Socrates* persuasively reads Plato's trilogy *Theaetetus*, *Sophist*, and *Statesman* as a comprehensive response, *avant la lettre*, to the grave philosophical and political errors of Socrates' modern critics. Priou's discussions of apparitions and semblances in the *Sophist*, and of the necessarily stochastic and sophistical nature of statesmanship, are particularly illuminating. Serious students of Plato will want to read, and reread, this fine book.

—Jacob Howland, author of *Glaucon's Fate: History, Myth, and Character in Plato's* Republic

Defending Socrates, Alex Priou's study of Plato's trilogy achieves an all-too-rare combination of concision and depth. Clearly the product of sustained and fruitful reflection on these dialogues, the work is informed by Priou's similarly illuminating treatment of the *Parmenides* in his previous book and by his mastery of the Greek. Priou frames the trilogy as Socrates's examination of science. His understanding of those philosophic premises of science that are shared by its ancient and modern versions sheds new light on these dialogues. As Priou convincingly argues, the Socratic perspective lets us see how modern science's reluctance to address the question of happiness has impoverished our self-understanding and made the recurrence to this ancient wisdom all the more urgent and necessary. Not only for students of Plato but for anyone who wishes to understand better the ground on which we stand, *Defending Socrates* is a book not to be missed.

—Paul Stern, Ursinus College

MERCER UNIVERSITY PRESS

Endowed by

TOM WATSON BROWN
and
THE WATSON-BROWN FOUNDATION, INC.

DEFENDING SOCRATES

Political Philosophy Before the Tribunal of Science

Alex Priou

MERCER UNIVERSITY PRESS
Macon, Georgia

MUP/ P685

© 2023 by Mercer University Press
Published by Mercer University Press
1501 Mercer University Drive
Macon, Georgia 31207
All rights reserved

27 26 25 24 23   5 4 3 2 1

Books published by Mercer University Press are printed on acid-free paper that meets the requirements of the American National Standard for Information Sciences—Permanence of Paper for Printed Library Materials.

Printed and bound in the United States.

This book is set in Adobe Caslon.

Cover/jacket design by Burt&Burt.

ISBN   978-0-88146-914-1
Cataloging-in-Publication Data is available from the Library of Congress

For Ronna Burger

ἡ δὲ φιλοσοφία ἀεὶ τῶν αὐτῶν, λέγει δὲ ἃ σὺ νῦν θαυμάζεις.

—Plato, *Gorgias* 482a7–b1

CONTENTS

Acknowledgments | viii

Overture | 1

1. Theaetetus | 21

2. Sophist | 53

3. Statesman | 93

4. "Theaetetus" | 137

Bibliography | 175

Index of Names | 183

Index of Ideas | 184

ACKNOWLEDGMENTS

Over the years of its genesis, this book has benefited from the insight of too many teachers, friends, panel discussants, reviewers, and editors to mention. Nevertheless, I must single out a few people in particular. I would like, first, to thank Marc Jolley and the editorial staff at Mercer University Press for their helpful guidance in ushering the manuscript to print. I must also thank my wife, Kristin, to whom I owe an unpayable debt. The long hours spent writing and editing, in addition to the inevitable unpredictability of mood that would result, have demanded of her more patience than it has been reasonable of me to expect. For that gift, my gratitude and love are poor compensation.

The greatest debt of gratitude, however, is owed to my graduate advisor Ronna Burger, whose terse and fruitful insights during her courses on Plato's trilogy have yielded far more than I could ever have expected upon first hearing. Most significant in the formation of the thesis of this work were two paradigm-shifting insights: first, the connection of Socrates' confession of failure at the beginning of the *Sophist* to the problem of false opinion in the *Theaetetus*; second, the observation that Socrates composed, via Euclides, the *Theaetetus* while in prison, and the significance of this fact for the first insight. This dramatic distillation of the trilogy provided the seed, from which the present work was generated. It is for this reason that I've dedicated it to her.

As the title suggests, this work is related to my first book, *Becoming Socrates*. At the end of that book, I offered some remarks on Plato's trilogy, which I here expand upon and revise. It is my hope that together these books will serve as a guide to readers puzzled as to why Plato had Parmenides bookend Socrates' life, or at least that portion of his life not including his most distinctive public deed, his trial and death.

Chapter Two originally appeared as "The Philosopher in Plato's *Sophist*" in *Hermathena* 195, 5–29 (published in 2017 with the date of 2013). Chapter Four originally appeared as "Plato's *Theaetetus* and the Absent *Philosopher*" in *The International Journal of the Platonic Tradition* 10 (2016), 151–67. Both, however, have been heavily revised in light of my more recent work on the trilogy, in addition to being adapted to their present context.

OVERTURE

In what sense is Socrates in need of defense? And political philosophy, the activity with whose discovery he is so often credited? Since the inception of the modern scientific project, whose explicit goal has been the mastery and possession of nature, we have grown accustomed to relying on human ingenuity and power much more than ever before, thereby raising man to new heights. Yet we have been able to do so only by virtue of a lowering of our self-understanding. Turning away from man's highest ambitions, of noble self-sacrifice or the disinterested pursuit of knowledge, we have harnessed instead our fear and greed, so that scientifically and politically our shared purpose has been the invention of such technologies as will allow us to live longer and more comfortable lives.[1] This reduction of human longing, and the good at which it aims, had the

---

[1] Hence Machiavelli writes that "truly it is a very natural and ordinary thing to desire to acquire, and always, when men do it who can, they will be praised or not blamed; but when they cannot, and wish to do it anyway, here lie the error and the blame," and likewise that "one can say this generally of men; that they are ungrateful, fickle, pretenders and dissemblers, evaders of danger, eager for gain" (*The Prince* chapters 3 and 17, from Mansfield 1998, 14–15, 66; see, also, chapter 17, Mansfield 1998, 67). Hobbes famously "put[s] for a general inclination of all mankind, a perpetual and restless desire of power after power, that ceaseth only in death" (*Leviathan* I.11, paragraph 2; see, also, paragraph 1). Likewise, he states that "the passions that incline men to peace are fear of death, desire of such things as are necessary to commodious living, and a hope by their industry to obtain them" (*Leviathan* I.13, paragraph 14). Consider, further, that for Locke it is the desire for property that leads men to leave the state of nature and, likewise, that Bacon and Descartes promote the new science as able to relieve us of our ills, including even that of death (see Locke, *Two Treatises of Government* II, §§40–45; Bacon's *Great Instauration*, in Bacon 2017, 16, 32; and compare Descartes, *Discourse on the Method* Part 6 with *The Passions of the Soul* Art. 176).

political effect of delegitimizing traditional hierarchies and the scientific effect of prioritizing, over other considerations, the material nature of things—that is, our bodies and the physical things around us. Common to both is the democratization of truth. We deem most true whatever alleviates our common physical fragility or increases our leisure, and does so demonstrably, that is, by an equally accessible and certain use of reason. To be sure, this democratization has had its benefits. It has arguably put at our disposal a greater proportion of our now longer lives. Yet it has done so at the price of making us skeptical that there are any standards, beyond individual whim, by which to judge whether that leisure is well-used and our lives well-lived. Every life, including the good life, is deemed idiosyncratic.[2] With the good so conceived, political philosophy came to be tolerated, a great achievement no doubt, but only by being much misunderstood, even maligned. All higher claims to the work of our hands and our minds came under increasing suspicion, with the way of life exemplified by Socrates deemed most foolish of all.[3] Athens

---

[2] "These words of good, evil, and contemptible," writes Hobbes, "are ever used with relation to the person that useth them, there being nothing simply and absolutely so, nor any common rule of good and evil to be taken from the nature of the objects themselves" (*Leviathan* I.6, paragraph 7). See, also, I.11, paragraph 1. Compare Bacon: "My next [admonition], that…they not fall into the opposite error, which they will surely do if they think that the inquisition of nature is in any part interdicted or forbidden. For it was not that pure and uncorrupted natural knowledge whereby Adam gave names to the creatures according to their propriety, which gave occasion to the fall. It was the ambitious and proud desire of moral knowledge to judge of good and evil, to the end that man may revolt from God and give laws to himself, which was the form and manner of the temptation" (*The Great Instauration*, in Bacon 2017, 17).

[3] Descartes subtly critiques Socrates in his dismissal of Socratic skepticism at the outset of the *Meditations*: "At last I will apply myself earnestly and unreservedly to this general demolition of my opinions. Yet to bring this about I will not need to show that all my opinions are false, which is perhaps something I could never accomplish…Nor therefore need I survey each opinion individually, a task that would be endless" (Descartes 1993, 13–14). Consider, too, his remarks on wonder in *The Passions of the Soul* Arts. 72–78. Spinoza is

may have put Socrates to death, but in so doing she allowed Plato to consecrate him as a martyr. It is rather we moderns who have sought, whether we know it or not, to nail the coffin shut.

We have achieved this closure on Socrates, and the way of life he modeled, only by virtue of a second trial conducted against him, in the name of science, nearly half a millennium ago. Though he was tried *in absentia*, still by nearly all witness accounts Socrates lost. Much like their Athenian counterparts, his modern accusers leveled two charges against him, which we can reconstruct along the following lines.

In the first place, they claimed, the Socratic method is simply unscientific—in truth, no method at all. Socrates always begins from ordinary opinion. Ordinary opinion, however, is based on ordinary experience, which relies in turn on the evidence of the senses. Yet doesn't ordinary experience also teach us that the senses are not to be trusted? The opinions with which Socrates begins are, therefore, hardly worth even thinking about, scientifically speaking. They are instead to be rejected out of hand. The proper starting point is rather

---

rather explicit in a letter to Hugo Boxel: "The authority of Plato, Aristotle and Socrates carries little weight with me. I should have been surprised if you had produced Epicurus, Democritus, Lucretius or one of the Atomists or defenders of the atoms. It is not surprising that those who have thought up occult qualities, intentional species, substantial forms and a thousand more bits of nonsense should have devised spectres and ghosts, and given credence to old wives' tales with view to disparaging the authority of Democritus, whose high reputation they so envied that they burned the books which he had published amidst so much acclaim" (Spinoza 1995, 279). Consider, further, Bacon, *Advancement of Learning* 2.23.49, among many other similar passages throughout the *New Organon*, and the apparent origin of this trend, Machiavelli, *The Prince* chapter 15. For another, interesting angle, consider Locke's short essay "Labor," in Locke 1993, 440–42. As its name suggests, Bacon's *New Organon* corrects the deficiencies he finds in ancient, Aristotelian logic. His emphasis on inductive reasoning, however, has the further effect of making philosophy democratic in its attention to the senses common to all men rather than the opinions that necessarily vary among the ranks of human beings and men, with some potentially more conducive to philosophy than others.

a deep skepticism about our senses. We must aspire, that is, to the utmost care in formulating our opinions about the world by developing aids to render the senses more precise.[4] We would thereby avoid the characteristic error of Socrates' use of inductive reasoning, which is at best sloppy and at worst sophistic. Reliable inductive reasoning proceeds on the basis of a comprehensive set of data and by means of a precise, mathematical method. Socrates, however, tended to argue on the basis of a single example, or at best of a few examples, and by means of a metaphorical application to the matter at hand, and a dubiously selective one at that. In short, Socratic argumentation is *ad hominem* when deductive and specious when inductive. Never is it *really* scientific.

In the second place, these accusers continued, Socratic political philosophy is unscientific not simply in method but also in subject matter. Political philosophy is concerned with ends, with categories like the good, the just, and the beautiful or noble, as well as their opposites, but about such things there can be no knowledge, only vague and varied opinions. The good, we suspect, is not subject to scientific demonstration but a matter of individual fancy, a subjective vision. We must therefore avoid Socrates' mistake of trying to understand such categories, that is, of trying to determine the good life or the good in truth. What we can know are rather those material objects we make by craft or artifice, due to the mechanical necessity guiding their operation. If we wish to understand natural beings, therefore, we need only approach them as machines.[5] We must

---

[4] Descartes, *Meditations* Meditations One and Two. See, also, Bacon, *The Great Instauration*, "The Plan of the Work," description of part two (Bacon 2017, 23–24).

[5] "So that those who do not know the force of mathematical demonstrations…will not attempt to deny [this account of the heart] without examination, I would like to inform them that the movement I have just explained follows as necessarily…as does the movement of a clock from the force arrangement, and shape of its counterweights and wheels" (Descartes, *Discourse on the Method* Part 5, in Descartes 2007, 42; compare *Meditations* Meditation Six, in Descartes 1993, 55–56). As the discussion of the *Statesman* will show,

focus simply on the mechanical necessity exhibited in nature, regardless of how we might use it for our own good. That is, we must seek the truth in abstraction from the good. At least thereby we will know our bodies and the things around us in such a way as to allow us to perfect the medical and technical arts. And, in any case, don't all of us readily admit that the power of these arts, and the health and comfort that issue therefrom, are self-evidently good?

Finding Socrates guilty on both charges, philosophy embarked on its attempt to mature into a science, that is, a mathematically precise natural science. This shift was at first small, in that it was confined to a few individuals with a special devotion to this emerging project. Yet its consequences have proven to be seismic. As the natural sciences advanced, their power to grant us health and ease of life grew indisputable. This had an inevitable charm on Europe, as sectarian war had left the philanthropic longings of much of its Christian population without an outlet. Charity became scientific, and so of this world.[6] Scientific innovation, in turn, became a valuable commodity, by which enterprising individuals might be able to

---

Young Socrates is an imperialist mathematician, Plato's anticipation, one could say, of the Cartesian (see Chapter III, Section II).

[6] Consider the beginning of Parts Two and Six of Descartes' *Discourse on the Method*, as well as Bacon's appropriation of the Fall in *The Great Instauration* and its second part, *The New Organon* (see, in this connection, note 2, above). Consider, also, Bacon's prayers and exhortations: "I most humbly and fervently pray to God the Father, God the Son, and God the Holy Ghost, that remembering the sorrows of mankind and the pilgrimage of this our life wherein we wear out days few and evil, they will vouchsafe *through my hands* to endow the human family with *new* mercies…we may not be wise above measure and sobriety but *cultivate truth in charity*" (Bacon, *Great Instauration*, in Bacon 2017, 16, emphasis added); "I would address one general admonition to all; that they consider what are the true ends of knowledge…and that they perfect and govern it in charity" (Bacon 2017, 17); "Humbly we pray that this mind may be steadfast in us, and that *through these our hands*, and the hands of others to whom thou shalt give the same spirit, thou wilt vouchsafe to endow the human family with *new* mercies" (Bacon, *Great Instauration*, in Bacon 2017, 32, emphasis added). See also *New Organon* II.52 (end).

enrich themselves. It was inevitable, therefore, that the modern hybrid of liberal economics and scientific innovation would emerge. Emerge it did, and more: it came to dominate the West and, in time, the world. The contemporary form of this development is a technologically advanced and deeply interconnected world economy, in which nearly every worker contributes either directly, as scientist or inventor, or indirectly, in support of them, to the project of mastering nature for the sake of easing our ills and magnifying our comforts. To maintain this massive political and economic regime, workers have been necessary, that is, workers educated to the point of extreme specialization and sophistication in the sciences. Consequently, our educational institutions have grown larger and more lop-sided toward the so-called STEM fields—Science, Technology, Engineering, and Mathematics. To persuade students down this path, the public rhetoric surrounding education has placed much emphasis on the usefulness of one's degree, on earning potential and job stability, and on the outsized demand for certain specializations, in addition to the honor accruing to the discipline required and the generosity in sharing the fruits thereof. This shift has therefore had an inevitable effect on what it means to be well-educated, as interest in the Humanities has steadily dwindled among students, to the point of near extinction.

We should hardly be surprised at the decay of interest in those disciplines treating the human things, following as it necessarily does from our dismissal or tabling of the question of the good life, the central question of Socratic political philosophy. This decay is but Socrates' second death, that of the tradition he initiated. Of course, we ought not lament when the sun finally sets on a long error. Why even call this evening respite a "decay"? Didn't Socrates lose his scientific trial? What is this tradition, really, but a parade of deformed offspring, sired by unscientific men unjustly claiming to know the unknowable? All these books on the good, and from them no measurable good. We should lament much more if they continue to be read. How much good, by comparison, has come from modern natural science and technology? Are we not today immeasurably happier than our forebears? Do we not, at any rate, live longer and in greater comfort? The history of philosophy may be, as Alfred North Whitehead famously declared, a series of footnotes to Plato; but if, for the scientist today, philosophy is dead, then Plato is a footnote in the history of science and, what's more, a non-entity for the present.[7]

It is here, on the question of happiness, that the case against Socrates grows suspect. The founders of modernity set their sights on satisfying what is most common in human nature, our material needs. Toward that end, they focused on the operation of our bodies and the bodies of the things around us, the mechanics of a thing rather than its end or good, that is, the ultimate purpose guiding its organization and operation. This abstraction has cut two ways. It has, of course, unleashed immense powers to preserve and delight us, to keep us alive and keep us pleased. But it has done so only by defaming those aforementioned higher claims to our time and energy. And it is for this reason that the conveniences of modern life have proven unsatisfying to our deeper longings. Is it really a matter of chance that, by organizing politics and education around mere preservation and convenience, we have left ourselves unfulfilled? Whereas the ancient philosophers spoke of love, wonder, and happiness, our philosophers speak of boredom, anxiety, and despair. But what else should we expect from tabling the question of the highest good so as to ascertain the low but true, the basest truth and it alone? If the great experiment of modernity has taught us anything about the human good, it is that we want our place in the whole to consist of something more than mere material satisfaction.

But so what if we *want* more? Does wanting alone suffice to demonstrate the possibility of what's wanted? Yes, we have abstracted from the good in order to approach the true and, yes, this

---

[7] See Hawking 2010, 5. For a "Platonic" understanding of physical laws, see the passing remarks on miracles and beauty in Penrose 2010. Hawking criticizes Penrose for his Platonism in Hawking and Penrose 1996, 3–4 with 134–35. Penrose is much more sensitive to the charm of the beautiful, and the implications thereof, than is Hawking.

has left human life unmoored and unsatisfying. But might this not be the hard truth at the end of history, of this "highway of despair," the irrationality at the end of reason, namely, that we are driven by ambitions that reality cannot satisfy? Is it not still the case that philosophy has matured into a science and that this science has discovered the truth, in all its stubborn ugliness? This line of reasoning, advanced by Socrates' latest accusers, is not without its merits, but it differs from the line advanced by his earlier accusers. Paradoxically, they abstracted from the good for the sake of the good, that is, for the sake of the material goods provided by artifice. The hope then was that most might find happiness in a life of comfortable contentment, while the ambitious few might seek honor and glory in scientific discovery.[8] Men have refused, however, to be so mollified. The initial project is thus open to suspicion on the grounds of the question of the good life, the very question that project's proponents claimed to have abstracted from yet quietly invoked. Our descent into nihilism may be a creature of modernity and not borne of an unassailable insight into the human condition as such. Socrates' conviction before the tribunal of science may therefore be owed to his absence, to his being tried *in absentia*—to the fact that he could not ask questions of his accusers. Regardless, his trial was poorly adjudicated; he deserves to have his case reheard. If justice toward Socrates does not move us here, then the possibility of living happily in the modern world certainly should.—

Where, then, are we to turn for a scientific accusation against Socrates, in which Socrates is not denied his say? We might reasonably turn to Plato's own writing on the question of knowledge or science (ἐπιστήμη), the *Theaetetus*. Very much to our purposes, Socrates conducts this conversation with some scientific men, the mathematician and astronomer Theodorus and his brightest student,

---

[8] These few sentences are meant to condense the regime of Bensalem in Bacon's *The New Atlantis*.

Athenian or otherwise, Theaetetus (*Theaetetus* 144a1–3).[9] Theaetetus first answers the question, What is knowledge?, with a list of sciences or areas of knowledge (ἐπιστῆμαι) that he has studied with Theodorus, such disciplines as geometry and astronomy, among others (*Theaetetus* 146c7–d3). When pressed to define knowledge as a whole, however, Theaetetus retreats into a position similar to that of the sophist Protagoras, according to which what appears true to each person *is* true for him (*Theaetetus* 151e8–152a8).[10] Perception alone makes for knowledge (*Theaetetus* 151d7–e7). This is evident, we are told, from the variety of conventions concerning the good, the just, and the beautiful or noble (τὸ καλόν), a variety that suggests they are a matter of private perception on the part of an individual or a political community (*Theaetetus* 172a1–5). Socrates impressively counters this claim, advanced in the name of the sophist Protagoras, by arguing that what we perceive to be good often turns out not to be such when attained, suggesting therefore that there is an experientially verifiable distinction between apparent goods and true goods (*Theaetetus* 172a5–b8, 177c6–179d1). Knowledge is therefore to be found, if anywhere, not in mere perception but in the gathering-together (συλλογισμός) or gathering-up (ἀναλογισμός) of our perceptions, that is, in the sense we make of them (*Theaetetus* 186b11–d6). Socrates seems, therefore, to have justified the possibility of political philosophy over and against the

---

[9] Unless noted otherwise, all citations without an author are to Plato. All translations are my own. For my translations and citations of the trilogy, I have used the text of Duke et al. 1995 and consulted the translation of Benardete 1984. For the fragments of Parmenides and Heraclitus, I have used the text of Coxon 2009 and Marcovich 1967, respectively, but in the case of both I have used the traditional Diels-Kranz numbering.

[10] The *Protagoras* ends with the question whether virtue can be knowledge while not being teachable, as Socrates maintains. This issue is latent in the *Theaetetus*, where Socrates attempts to have Theaetetus look beyond the mathematical or teachable things to another account of knowledge (see Chapter IV, Section III). It is only late in life, then, that Socrates returns to the question that remained at the end of his conversation with Protagoras.

critique that, because the good is a matter of individual fancy, its examination belongs rather to the realm of sophistry (see *Theaetetus* 165e8–168c2). But when it comes time for Socrates and Theaetetus to determine what this gathering-together or gathering-up is—whatever it is knowledge might be, *beyond* perception—they find themselves unable to come up with an adequate answer. Their final definition of knowledge is that it is a true opinion accompanied by an account that tethers that opinion to reality, to the being under examination (*Theaetetus* 206c1–8, 206e6–207a1, 208c4–8). Yet none of the descriptions they entertain, of how speech relates to being, proves satisfactory (*Theaetetus* 210a3–b7). On first glance, therefore, the *Theaetetus* appears to corroborate the verdict of Socrates' scientific trial in early modernity. Socrates was unable to demonstrate the possibility of political philosophy's inquiry into the good in truth. He is guilty of sophistry, be it voluntary or not.

That is, at least, how Theodorus takes it. At the end of their conversation, Socrates suggests that they meet up again on the following day, as indeed they do in the *Sophist*, presumably to complete or at least continue their unfinished inquiry (*Sophist* 216a1–2 with *Theaetetus* 210d2–4). Unexpectedly, however, Theodorus brings with him "a very philosophic man" with a prestigious philosophic pedigree, an anonymous Stranger from the city of Elea and member of the circle around Parmenides (*Sophist* 216a2–4). Theodorus appears to have brought the Stranger along because he believes Socrates is in need of some assistance, if not correction, in his inquiry. In response, Socrates somewhat playfully suggests that the Stranger may really be a refutative or reproachful god (θεός...τις ἐλεγκτικός), come to visit upon them his punitive providence (*Sophist* 216b3–6). But Theodorus again departs from Socrates, this time as regards the very nature of philosophy, seeing the refutation (ἔλεγχος) of which Socrates spoke as a sort of strife (ἔρις) (*Sophist* 216b3–8). Theodorus clearly has in mind his experience (πάθος) of Socrates the day before in the *Theaetetus*, where he was repeatedly dragged into the conversation against his will—almost criminally, in his mind—and primarily in order to assent to a devastating critique of his deceased friend Protagoras (see *Theaetetus* 169a6–b4). When, after a long discussion, Socrates finally let Theodorus go, Theodorus never spoke again in this dialogue. That the *Theaetetus* was inconclusive on its guiding question, What is knowledge?, appears to have made Theodorus ask, "To what end did I endure Socrates' abuse?" It is with these experiences in mind, it would seem, that Theodorus introduces the Stranger as more measured (μετριώτερος) than those who, like Socrates, engage in eristic, strife-ridden speech (*Sophist* 216b7–c1). Whatever Socrates may have had in mind in proposing they meet up again, Theodorus appears to have viewed it as an opportunity to put Socrates in his place.

At the heart of Theodorus' misgivings about Socratic refutation as needlessly combative is the conviction that sophistry and philosophy can and should be entirely separate. And while Socrates does adopt Theodorus' tone of disappointment at their conversation of the day before, he nevertheless maintains that the philosopher cannot avoid assuming the distortive apparitions (φαντάσματα) of the sophist and statesman because of the ignorance of others (*Sophist* 216c4–5: διὰ τὴν τῶν ἄλλων ἄγνοιαν; see *Theaetetus* 164c8–d2). What's more, the language in which Socrates expresses his fear that the Stranger may be a refutative God there to punish them for being paltry (φαύλους) in speeches refers not so much to their failure to define what knowledge is as it does to their failure to define false opinion adequately (*Sophist* 216b4–6, *Theaetetus* 196d2–12, esp. d8: πᾶς ἡμῖν ἐξ ἀρχῆς ὁ λόγος, 197a3–4: φαῦλοι). Certainly this failure is noteworthy. For, in the absence of a definition of false opinion, could Socrates really justify what he often appears to be doing, namely, purifying his interlocutors' souls of false opinions so as to guide them to true ones? However we answer, we are further impressed that the Stranger not only appears to succeed where Theodorus deemed Socrates to have failed, namely, by separating the sophist from the philosopher to Theodorus' satisfaction; he also appears to succeed precisely where Socrates deemed himself to have failed, namely, in defining false opinion. The Stranger would therefore have made good on Theodorus' critique of Socrates, both by modeling a more measured or moderate form of philosophy and by showing Socrates that he dabbled needlessly in sophistry. Theodorus was right, it appears, to accuse Socrates of criminality. Not just the *Theaetetus*, then, but its sequels in this trilogy, the *Sophist* and *Statesman*, appear to confirm the judgment of Socrates' early modern critics against him. Once again, Socrates appears to be a sophist.

We cannot help but find this interpretation of Plato's trilogy dissatisfying, based as it is on a reading of the *Theaetetus* that no scholar would ever find persuasive—no scholar, that is, save Theodorus. But Theodorus is not a philosopher or political philosopher, nor a modern scholar of Greek philosophy and political philosophy, but a mathematician and natural scientist through-and-through. As he repeatedly reminds us, he has no inclination toward Socrates' manner of inquiry nor even toward Socrates himself: it is Socrates who went to Theodorus in search of talented students—Theodorus did not bring his best to Socrates. So, why would Theodorus' modern kinsmen act any differently than he, and voluntarily go to Socrates? His modern trial, we recall, was conducted *in absentia*. It is unsurprising, therefore, that Theodorus' reading of the *Theaetetus* should find no advocates in the disciplines devoted to the study of Plato. But this is only to say that the scholarship reflects a self-selection bias. Ultimately, it is undeniable that this is the backdrop Plato gives the trilogy: Theodorus *does* read the conversation in the *Theaetetus* as a failure and *does* judge Socrates as to blame, and the Stranger *does* follow Theodorus' lead in offering an alternative to Socratic philosophy. Though scholars are little inclined to model their understanding of Socrates on Theodorus, however friendly they may be to the Stranger, still we must put ourselves in Theodorus' shoes if we are to understand the spirit in which the Stranger offers the critique of Socrates found in the *Sophist* and *Statesman*, a spirit that manifestly emerges from Theodorus. That is, we must attempt to read the *Theaetetus* not as scholars of philosophy or political philosophy, sensitive to the ambiguities inherent in the subject matter, but with a bias toward demonstrative science as *the* model of knowledge—more specifically, as an older scientific man stuck in his ways, uninclined and even hostile to Socratic refutation. Much as it may pain us, we must try to *be* Theodorus.

Reading Plato's trilogy in this way of course leaves one thing out, for our purposes: the Socratic response to what I will refer to as the Stranger's Theodoran critique of Socrates in the *Sophist* and *Statesman*. This response, I believe, is contained in the *Theaetetus*. It might sound strange, even absurd, to take the earlier conversation to be a response to the later, but in a crucial way the earlier conversation *is* later, since Plato presents it as having been composed *after* the *Sophist* and *Statesman*. At the end of the *Theaetetus*, Socrates informs Theodorus that they must reconvene the next day because now Socrates has to go to the court of the king to receive Meletus' indictment of him, the very indictment that would ultimately lead to Socrates' trial, imprisonment, and death, as presented in the *Euthyphro*, *Apology of Socrates*, *Crito*, and *Phaedo* (see *Theaetetus* 210d2–4, *Sophist* 216a1–2). At some point during this series of events a Megarian named Euclides visited Socrates with some frequency to record the conversation found in the *Theaetetus* (*Theaetetus* 142c8–143a7). Whether Euclides visited Socrates while he was awaiting his trial or his death is unclear, so that we do not know whether it was recorded with Socrates aware or unaware of the Athenian jurors' judgment on and of his life. But Euclides' presence at Socrates' death and absence from his trial suggest that it was during Socrates' imprisonment that Euclides especially frequented him, as Phaedo's comments also suggest (see *Phaedo* 59c1–3, d1–2). Socrates' conviction and sentence would surely have made such visits especially urgent, for with the departure of Socrates goes also his testimony. Still, whatever the case, Socrates composed the *Theaetetus* via proxy *after* the *Sophist* and *Statesman*, in full awareness of the Stranger's Theodoran critique. We are invited, then, to read the *Theaetetus* both before and after the *Sophist* and *Statesman*. That much is clear.

Less clear, but also essential, is the question why Socrates indulged Euclides' interest in this conversation at all, why he took such pains to have it preserved. At the beginning of the *Sophist*, and again at the beginning of the *Statesman*, the group anticipates that, after defining the sophist in the *Sophist* and the statesman in the *Statesman*, they will go on to define the philosopher in, we assume, the *Philosopher*. Plato thus suggests, by situating the *Theaetetus* both before and after the *Sophist* and *Statesman*, that the *Theaetetus*, when read as a response to the Stranger's critique, rather than as inviting it, replaces the unwritten but anticipated fourth dialogue, the *Philosopher*. The suggestion, in other words, is that what we witness in the *Theaetetus* is not philosophic failure but the philosopher *par excellence*.[11] It promises, in other words, to correct the mistaken, Theodoran reading of the *Theaetetus* and therewith the critique it prompted in the *Sophist* and *Statesman*. That is the hope, at least. At a minimum, the Socrates of the *Theaetetus* admits of two readings. There is, first, Socrates the character, inside the dialogue's action and on its stage, who attempts to save the young Theaetetus from the clutches of the sophist Protagoras, only eventually to earn the title of sophist himself, in what looks conspicuously like the

---

[11] There are a few theories and claims about why we do not have a dialogue titled the *Philosopher*. Howland argues that the trial itself is to take its place (Howland 1998, 8; but see also 226–27), while Leibowitz claims in passing that the *Apology of Socrates* alone takes its place (Leibowitz 2010, 3), as does Bartlett (Bartlett 2017, 247–48). Benardete and Notomi both suggest it is to be found in the *Sophist* and *Statesman*, albeit for very different reasons (see Benardete 2000, 328–29; Notomi 2017, esp. 193). I agree with Cropsey, who speculates that the *Theaetetus* takes its place (Cropsey 1995, 30), though the *Theaetetus* on my reading both precedes and follows the *Sophist* and *Statesman*. For a helpful summary of views, see Gill 2012, 1 n. 3. I will not address each view, but rather allow my case to speak for itself. That said, as the *Apology of Socrates* comes directly after the *Statesman* in Plato's dramatic chronology and, in addition, has the name of a philosopher in its title, the claim of Leibowitz and those in agreement with him deserves special attention. I have addressed it in Chapter IV, at the beginning of Section I and again more briefly at the end of Section III.

tragedy of political philosophy. It is to this Socrates that Theodorus reacts in the *Sophist*. But there is also Socrates the author or poet, outside the text, unfolding and reflecting on his discursive decisions at a critical distance. But how, we wonder, does Socrates stand in relation to his written self? Is it as Sophocles stands to his Oedipus—never in danger of falling wholly into the plot—or as the self-blinded Oedipus stands to his infant self—thinking about what was and imagining what should have been, in the grips of reflective lamentation (see Sophocles, *Oedipus Tyrannus* 1349–55, 1391–1412, 1451–54)? That is, did Socrates see a response to the Stranger's apparent alternative in the way he had lived his life prior to his encounter with him, and embed that response in the *Theaetetus as written*? Did he show therein how the tragic understanding of Socrates is more a creature of Theodorus and Theaetetus' expectations of Socratic conversation than of the man himself?

We are guided in our inquiry, therefore, to read the *Theaetetus*, first, with all the flat-footedness of Theodorus, without a touch of irony or humor and with an eye to discerning the cause of his thinly-veiled contempt for Socrates at the outset of the *Sophist*. We must then read the *Sophist* and *Statesman* as the Stranger's elaboration of the grounds of Theodorus' discontent. Crucial to our understanding of the Stranger will be his indications that the Theodoran critique of Socrates that he advances fulfills the demands *not* of truth but of justice—indeed, the divine justice of Zeus. That is, hearing Socrates' references to Zeus' law of ξενία or guest-friendship, the Stranger expresses concern that he—the Stranger—not act toward Theodorus with the savagery Antinous shared with his Cycloptic predecessor Polyphemus, but rather fulfill the elder mathematician's expectation of a more moderate or measured (μετριώτερος) alternative to Socratic philosophy.[12] He is not to plunder Theodorus' home.

---

[12] Compare *Sophist* 216a1–218a1 with Homer, *Odyssey* 2.17–20, 7.186–206, 9.166–76, 212–15, 252–80, 17.364–465, 20.1–21. See, also, note 36 in Chapter 3. Note, lastly, that Socrates changes Theodorus' κατὰ τὴν χθὲς ὁμολογίαν (216a1) to κατὰ τὸν Ὁμήρου λόγον (216a6). The λόγος of

The Stranger thus attempts to satisfy his host Theodorus with a putative separation of these three men—that is, the sophist, statesman, and philosopher—only to show Socrates (over Theodorus and his young students' heads) that they are inextricably bound up with one another. The Stranger thus manages to satisfy both men by hiding his transgression of Zeus' law beneath the veneer of reverent fear (see *Sophist* 217d8: αἰδώς with 216b1: αἰδοῦς). As the allusions to the *Odyssey* show, I believe, he is rather in fundamental agreement with Socrates from the very beginning.[13] After detailing how the

---

Homer displays the law of Zeus. See the next note, as well as my essay, "Olympus as Hades," forthcoming in a volume on Parmenides edited by Colin Smith.

[13] There is some debate surrounding the extent of the Stranger's irony. Many have noted that the Stranger's deeds contradict his speeches, but only some have viewed it as deliberate. Howland, for example, refers to the Stranger as flattering Theodorus (Howland 1998, 168), though also as a critic of Socrates (Howland 1998, 3), whereas Zuckert sees the Stranger as posing a challenge to Socrates and Socrates' trial and death as responding to that challenge (Zuckert 2009, 596–97, 681). Dinan charts a middle course, in that he sees the Stranger as effecting a Socratic turn when he encounters a version of Socratic cathartics in the fifth sophist (Dinan 2013, 117–21); so, too, does Rosen, who argues that, "in carrying out his effort to punish Socrates, the Stranger comes closer and closer to Socratic doctrine, until finally, despite all differences in character and rhetoric, one can scarcely distinguish between the contents of their speeches" (Rosen 1979, 8; see, also, Rosen 1983, 25), with whom Hyland also agrees (see Hyland 2015 and 2017). Hopkins provides a provocative argument for the unity of Socrates and the Stranger by focusing on "the mathematical context of each of the [trilogy's] dialogues in relation to their central philosophical concerns" (see Hopkins 2017, 270 and 282). Closer to my interpretation is Umphrey's view that "the Stranger appears to have undertaken a second sailing. No one would mistake him for a pre-Socratic natural philosopher, and his semantic-extensionalist turn sets him apart from Parmenides and Zeno as well. The *Sophist* and *Statesman* display the Socratic turn modified. One could hardly find a better illustration of the slipperiness of likenesses than in the resemblance between Plato's Eleatic Stranger and Plato's Socrates as philosophers" (Umphrey 2018, 62). This may or may not be the same position that Benardete takes in his late writings on the trilogy. Of the *Sophist*, he writes that "the Stranger's art of hunting does seem to be

Stranger does this in the *Sophist* and *Statesman*, we must then return to the *Theaetetus* with Socrates' ironic eye, looking to see how Socrates' record of his actual conduct absolves him both of Theodorus' accusation and the Stranger's more substantive critique, that Socrates is contentious in a manner unbefitting a philosopher. The *Theaetetus* thus shows us both the cause of Theodorus' discontent and Socrates' reasons for so upsetting him. It is Socrates' meditation on the necessity of his being misunderstood.[14] As we will see, therefore, this second, more robust, and ironic reading of the *Theaetetus* will expose the *Sophist* and *Statesman* as two more tragedies, in addition

---

due to phantastics, for it seems to be adjusted to Theaetetus, who is to pass for manly and brave in following the track of the sophist"; likewise, in the *Statesman* "what might seem to be the pushiness of politics, as if it wanted to give itself the airs of a theoretical science, is really the Stranger's indulgence of Theodorus's desire to punish Socrates for letting him down" (Benardete 2000, 337, 355). That is, in both dialogues Benardete sees the Stranger as consciously employing a mode of φανταστική. In Umphrey's words, "the Stranger divides not only in accordance with eidetic differences…but also in accordance with the abilities and limitations of his interlocutors" (Umphrey 2019, 63). The basic question is whether the Stranger really intends to offer an alternative to Socratic philosophy, as he appears to do, or rather adopts this as an ironic pose. The matter appears to me to be settled by the subtle allusions to the *Odyssey*. Socrates calls for him and Theodorus to honor the bonds of ξενία or guest-friendship (*Sophist* 216a5–b6). Theodorus misses the point (*Sophist* 216b7–c1), but not the Stranger, who gratifies the group so as not to appear ἄξενον and ἄγριον—so as not to treat them as Odysseus was by Polyphemus and, later, Antinous (see note 12). The Stranger sees himself as compelled to find a way to gratify Theodorus and Socrates at once—the former by presenting philosophy in a more measured or moderate form, the latter by doing so while guiding the overly measured or moderate Theaetetus. From the very beginning, then, the Stranger is wholly aware of his circumstances and, more importantly, adapts himself to suit them. This is his practice of φανταστική. See, also, note 36 to chapter III..

[14] "Notwithstanding Euclides' modifications, the text provides as close to a Socratic self-portrait as occurs in any dialogue"; but "the self-portrait lacks photographic clarity. Socrates' valedictory leaves a legacy of perplexity" (Stern 2008, 29).—For the dating of these late dialogues, see Nails 2002, 321–23.

to the first, tragic reading of the *Theaetetus*. It is tempting, therefore, to read this sequence of four dialogues—*Theaetetus, Sophist, Statesman*, and "*Theaetetus*" again, but as the missing *Philosopher*—as a trilogy of tragedies followed by a light-hearted satyr play. Socrates does remark, in the *Phaedo*, that he spent his final days in prison writing poetry, among which he may have counted the *Theaetetus* (see *Phaedo* 60c9–61c1). It is left to us to decide its genre.

It is the task of this book to flesh out the above, skeletal interpretation of these dialogues as far as is necessary to exhibit how they serve as an ancient corollary to Socrates' scientific trial in early modernity.[15] It is a trial that places science center stage in its all-too-human context, a context populated by sophists both suspicious and enchanting, politicians either petty or stately, and a philosopher so protean that, in refusing to give his final word on anything, he escapes our final word on him. *This* Plato—too elusive for the scientist to turn him into a footnote—has us inquire into what it is about reality, and about us, that allows for this range. Why does the sophist charm us even as he frustrates us, the statesman evoke both our ire and our admiration, and the philosopher variously don the garb of doctor of soul, Achillean gadfly of Athens, midwife to pregnant boys, and pro bono pickup artist for pederasts (in the *Charmides, Apology of Socrates, Theaetetus,* and *Lysis*, respectively)? Plato's meditation on *science* in every instance points to our shared *ignorance* as the cause, with the triumvirate of sophist, statesman, and philosopher serving as a necessary phenomenon that eludes the animating spirit of science. As the Stranger laments to Young Socrates, "each of us runs the risk of knowing everything as if in a dream and then again is ignorant of everything as it is in waking" (*Statesman* 277d2–

---

[15] Howland interprets Socrates' philosophic trial as including the *Euthyphro* and *Cratylus* (Howland 1998, vii). Moreover, he notes that the *Cratylus, Sophist,* and *Statesman* "occupy that place in the story of Socrates' last days left vacant by the omitted proceedings connected with Meletus's indictment and the prosecution phase of the public trial" (Howland 1998, 3). Miller, too, sees these dialogues as a philosophic trial (Miller 2004, 2). I differ in placing emphasis on the fact that philosophy here is understood *scientifically*.

4).[16] Plato ultimately compels us to view the pursuit of knowledge as inseparable from considerations, first, of beauty and nobility and, thereafter, of law and regime, thereby positioning science, the attempt to know the beings with certainty, and accordingly epistemology and ontology, as subfields of the study of politics.[17] In short, Plato guides us to see why we cannot consider the good life but as the good in truth. With the unexpected discovery that political life has saturated all inquiry, political philosophy will emerge not only as possible but also as necessary. In being the science both first in urgency and first in rank, it will be both first for us and first simply (see Aristotle, *Nicomachean Ethics* I.4.1095b2–13).

---

[16] See Benardete 2000, 375 n. 11.

[17] For the *Theaetetus* as a work of political philosophy, see especially Stern 2018. On the trilogy as a whole as a meditation on science, see Strauss 1987, 68–69.

I

THEAETETUS

I.

The conversation Euclides' slave reads in the *Theaetetus* begins abruptly with Socrates asking Theodorus for the most promising (ἐπίδοξοι γενέσθαι ἐπιεικεῖς) youths *not* from Theodorus' city of Cyrene but from Socrates' own Athens (143d1–6).[1] Theodorus is quite clear that from among his students—Athenian or otherwise—it is Theaetetus who has a nature wondrously good, who proves the preeminently able and eager learner—remarkable, above all, in his combination of gentleness and manliness (143e4–144b6, 144d1). Theodorus' testimony is supported by subsequent events on the battlefield, as well as the corroborating document of Book X of Euclid's *Elements*, where we have enduring evidence of Theaetetus' impressive accomplishments in mathematics. And the conversations that follow also corroborate Theodorus' testimony to some degree, as Theaetetus traverses some rather difficult terrain with both Socrates and the Eleatic Stranger. But the superlative courage or manliness (ἀνδρεῖον παρ' ὁντινοῦν) he attributes to Theaetetus seems hyperbolic, for the young Athenian consistently proves deficient in eagerness (προθυμία) and thus requires constant encouragement from Socrates.[2] Whatever manliness he may have evinced—either before

---

[1] Unless noted otherwise, all references in this chapter are to the *Theaetetus*.

[2] Paying attention to the use of forms of πρόθυμος is helpful for tracking Socrates' progress with Theaetetus: the dialogue begins with a juxtaposition

Theodorus in geometry or before his compatriots on the battlefield—it does not appear to have played much of a role in *these* conversations. For, despite having heard of Socrates' questions from others, Theaetetus in his dizzied perplexity never sought Socrates out: Socrates had to seek out Theaetetus (148e1–5, 143d1–e2).

Theaetetus' peculiarly narrow cowardice appears of a piece with the shortcomings of his teacher Theodorus, who never hides how burdensome he finds Socratic inquiry (see 146b1–6, 162a4–c2, 164e2–165b5, 168c2–169c8, 171c8–9, 173b7–c6, 177c3–5, 183b7–d9). Nevertheless, Theaetetus possesses it to a significantly lesser degree, as he still has the concern (τὸ μέλειν) for Socrates' questions that Theodorus admits he lost long ago (148e6, 164e8–165a3). Both geometers suffer from the same sickness: possession by the ghost of Protagoras, a friend and comrade to Theodorus and, through frequent study, an intellectual influence on Theaetetus (152a5, 162a4, 171c8). Epistemic relativism, it would seem, appeals to these isolationist mathematicians, who observe that no answer to the question, What is knowledge?, meets their criterion of precision, however much that relativism may also threaten their own studies. They would sooner retreat to a disunified list of sciences, such as Theaetetus initially offers as a "definition" of knowledge (146c7–

---

of Theaetetus' eagerness to study geometry, astronomy, harmony, and calculation with Theodorus, on the one hand, and his eagerness to investigate whether Theodorus has knowledge of soul with Socrates, on the other (145b2, 3, d3); Socrates underscores his own eagerness for conversation (146a7); Theaetetus says he is eager to know what knowledge is, despite his skepticism (148d1, 3); Socrates' presentation of midwifery includes an exhortation to be eager to answer, which Theaetetus subsequently echoes (151c2, d8); a maidservant laughs at Thales' eagerness to know the heavens and ignorance of what is at his feet (174a7); Socrates remarks on the need to correct their prior eagerness when claiming knowledge is perception, that is, Theaetetus' eagerly delivered first definition (183a3); Socrates comments on Theaetetus' eager revision of his third definition shortly after giving it (187b9); in an example, Socrates mentions the eagerness to identify things from afar (193c2); and, finally, Theaetetus eagerly proposes that a whole of parts is different from an aggregate of parts (204b2–3, 4).

d4), than venture to understand the problem of science as such. Our hero Socrates thus travels to the geometers to free the promising young Theaetetus—on the cusp of his distinctive discoveries—by purging him of Protagoras' ghost in an act of philosophic exorcism.[3]

It is with Socrates so positioned that Plato unfolds the tragedy of the *Theaetetus*, and so guides our present retelling. Our concern in this chapter will primarily be to prepare ourselves for Theodorus' accusation and Socrates' own confession of failure at the outset of the *Sophist*, so as better to understand how the *Sophist* and *Statesman* constitute a response to Socrates' tragic fall in the *Theaetetus*. The reader must always bear in mind that such a reading tells at best only half the *Theaetetus*' story—a half that, like Theodorus, is dour and serious, altogether lacking in playfulness, but still every bit as essential to understanding its place in the trilogy as the more playful, ironic reading we will advance in Chapter Four. In Act One (covered in Section II), Socrates encounters the apparition of Protagoras in Theaetetus' first definition of knowledge as perception. In Scene One, Socrates revives and fortifies Protagoras to grand proportions, only to slay the newly emboldened sophist in Scene Two, and so purge the possessed Theaetetus. But in Act Two (Section III), Protagoras enjoys his revenge in Socrates' tragic fall. For in Scene One, our hero proves unable to distinguish between true and false opinions adequately, so that the privacy of perception extends to all opinions in a surprising return to Protagorean relativism; while in Scene Two, every attempt to tether true opinion to reality by means of an account (λόγος) fails, bringing Socrates to the conclusion that his celebration of philosophic freedom from the city's petty and narrow concerns was but a cave-dweller's dream. A brief and somber epilogue (Section IV) confirms Socrates' subservience to the city in his urgent departure to receive his indictment, and so sets the stage for

---

[3] Knorr compellingly argues that the problem Theaetetus describes in the *Theaetetus* will eventually bring him to make his later discoveries, as found in Euclid's *Elements* (see Knorr 1975, 299–300).

his unexpected encounter with the Eleatic Stranger on the following day.

II.

As mentioned, Act One of Plato's *Theaetetus* consists of Socrates' confrontation with and victory over Protagoras—his rise before his tragic fall. Scene One features Socrates' encounter with Protagoras' ghost in Theaetetus' skeptical definition of knowledge as perception. After reviving Protagoras and raising him to new heights, Socrates spends Scene Two in a dialectical swordfight with the sophist, ultimately defeating his longtime adversary in speech while singing his praise of philosophy. This heroic display certainly goes some way in encouraging the otherwise manly but on this question rather reluctant Theaetetus (148e1–6, 151d7–e1). For he is by its end possessed of a newfound eagerness, even holding his superiors accountable to their dialectical commitments (183b7–d9, 210b6–7). But such eagerness relies on Socrates' promise to deliver, as though a midwife, an opinion out of Theaetetus' concern (148e1–8)—so as either to purge him of a falsity and image (εἴδωλον) or to put in his possession his own bouncing baby truth (150a8–b2, b9–c3, e6–7, 151c2–4, d2–3). That is, Socrates assures Theaetetus that it is possible for philosophy to attain its object, truth—in this case, the truth of what knowledge is—unfathomable though this may seem to Theaetetus (148c9: Νὴ τὸν Δί[α]). Assuring his young companion that the fight will not be fought in vain, Socrates sets out to demonstrate for Theaetetus the possibility of philosophy against its skeptical adversary both in argument and by the example of his deed. To the extent that Socrates proves victorious in Act One, his celebratory song is no doubt merited. But again, Act Two will expose this victory for the spurious image it is, with Socrates emerging as a sort of Don Quixote, a self-stylized hero exalting as reality the phantoms of his mind.

Theaetetus

As soon as Theaetetus offers his first definition of knowledge as perception, Socrates suspects the influence of Protagoras—a suspicion immediately confirmed by Theaetetus himself (151e8–152a5). But much to Theaetetus' surprise, he channels not just Protagoras but all the wise, save Parmenides (152d2–e10). Theaetetus thus finds himself allied with the most illustrious minds of Greece, while Socrates must contend against a whole army of fluxists, marshalled by no less a general than Homer (153a1–3). Indeed, so impressed is Theaetetus with Socrates' celebration of his definition's virtues that now he cannot imagine *anyone* contending with what just moments ago he deemed too feeble even for utterance (153a4). But lest Theaetetus infer too quickly from his reversal of confidence a reversal of fortunes, Socrates impresses upon him that what this army would defeat is the veracity of his own science, mathematics (154c1–e6). For if knowledge is perception means that man is the measure of all things—that one's private perception is always true (153e4–155a5)—then the future author of *Elements* X will be no more an authority on incommensurables than a man who cannot count beyond twenty because he has only so many fingers and toes.[4] The tension in the argument reflects a tension in Theaetetus himself, who upon learning of this attack discovers that the argument on his tongue is at odds with the conviction of his mind, and so finds himself in the grips of dizzying perplexity (154c10–d2, 157d10–12, 158a8–b4). Theaetetus is not even one with himself (154a6–9). What Theaetetus ultimately fears losing is the sobriety and sanity of mathematics, a fear that no doubt drives his isolation to the mathematical sciences, but which is also related to his concern with Socrates' questions (154c10–d2). It is to this concern that Socrates appeals in enlisting him as his ally against their common foe lodged deep in Theaetetus' soul.

But Socrates first takes pains to embolden this foe to ever greater proportions. The most robust form Protagoras' view takes in

---

[4] On the sophists' tendency to mock mathematics, see Aristotle, *Metaphysics* B.2.996a32–b1, 997b34–998a6.

Scene One is in the passage running from 155d9 to 157c1. There, Socrates presents Protagoras as elaborating his doctrine of the privacy of perception (153e4–154a3) into a rather sophisticated ontology—or, rather, anti-ontology (see 157b1). According to *this* Protagoras, there are two forms, species, or "looks" (εἴδη) of motion, the one having the power (δύναμις) to do or make (ποιεῖν), the other to experience or suffer (πάσχειν) (156a3–7). The results of this interaction are limitless but always in line with this twofold division, with the consequence being that nothing is one in itself or is itself by itself, that is, that everything is what it is *only* in relation to another at that very moment (156a7–b2, 156e8–157a2, 8 with 152d2–3, 6, 182b3–4). Though Protagoras laments our use of the verb "to be," nevertheless "being" resides, if anywhere, in this momentary interplay of agent (τὸ ποιοῦν) and patient (τὸ πάσχον), so that whatever one perceives truly *is* so long as one perceives it, and only so long (157a7–b3 with 152c5–7; see 166c6). More precisely, though, all is in a state of constant becoming, doing or making, and destruction and alteration, and only such words as these are in accordance with nature (φύσις) (157b3–7). So impressively robust is Socrates' revival of Protagoras—his contradictory use of terms like species (εἶδος) and nature (φύσις) notwithstanding—that Theaetetus is willing to believe that Socrates himself is convinced of what he says (157c4–6). But lest Theaetetus get too far ahead of himself, Socrates immediately touches again upon Theaetetus' desire for some sobriety in the face of such an argument as would have the judgments of a madman be no less veracious than those of a mathematician (158a8–b4). Likewise, Socrates turns the argument against himself, by remarking that it robs him of his famous ignorance—what he here calls his "sterility" (150c4: ἄγονος, pun on ἄγνοια)—and makes him a knower no less (but also no more) than anyone else (160c7–d4, 167d2–4, 179a10–b5).[5] Socrates' sophisticated revival of Protagoras' ghost has taken down Theaetetus' science and Socrates' ignorance all in one stroke. It is on this gloomy note that Socrates completes his delivery of Theaetetus' child and abruptly warns him of his intention to hollow it out (160d5–161a4).

Socrates does not waste time, as the outset of Scene Two sees him take quickly to mockery. So quick is Socrates' attack that Theodorus, having interjected upon the delivery's completion to reiterate his confidence in Theaetetus, is in just a page taken aback by the severity of Socrates' assault on his dear friend Protagoras (161a5–6 with 162a4). But Socrates' attack is more hasty than swift and decisive, for he immediately finds himself being rebuked by "Protagoras" (162d3–163a1). These opening pages set the tone for the coming back-and-forth, where we will see Socrates first mocking, then sophistic, and finally driving dialectically to the ontological basis of Protagoras' position.

Socrates begins with two opening attacks. The first concerns the possibility of wisdom (σοφία) in the sense of expertise. If knowledge is perception, how can Protagoras claim to be more of an authority than a *pig* (161c5; compare *Statesman* 266c8)? How, that is, can Socrates' Protagoras claim to be wise, as indeed the real, living Protagoras did (even to Socrates' approval) (161d7–e3; *Protagoras* 317b3–4 with 309c9–d2, 317d7–8)? In response to this attack, Protagoras—always Socrates' "Protagoras"—rebukes Socrates *et alii* for their inexactness, which falls far short of the standards of demonstration (ἀπόδειξις) and necessity (ἀνάγκη) expected of geometers like Theodorus (162e5–163a1). He is right in his rebuke, for though his claim to expertise will be his downfall, still Socrates touches upon the matter only obliquely, by semblance (εἰκόσι), rather than driving to the basic premises of Protagoras' position and

---

[5] Socrates' playful example of the taste of wine while he is healthy or sick reminds, of course, of his death, and so connects the question of whether Socrates deserves his hemlock to that of his ability to escape Protagoras' argument (compare 159b2–160d4 with *Lysis* 219d2–e4).

showing that the problem lies therein. Socrates' mocking swipe is thus quickly swatted away. After Protagoras' rebuke, Socrates levels his second attack, this one focusing on the memory: Do we not know the things we remember as we remember them (163d1–4)? If knowledge is perception, it would appear that we know nothing when our eyes are closed. But isn't it unfathomable to say that, when we close our eyes and remember what we were just looking at, we don't know what we recall (163e12–164a6, esp. δεινόν and νὴ τὸν Δία)? Socrates concludes from this second attack that knowledge and perception are different, and so issues the guiding question, What is knowledge?, once again (164b8–c2). But here, too, he proves too hasty, as he stops himself—this time as Socrates rather than as "Protagoras"—before Theaetetus can offer a new definition (or, as is more likely, balk again). Admitting to the very defect that Theodorus will cite on the following day—namely, that Socrates speaks primarily in strife (*Sophist* 216b8: τὰς ἔριδας)—Socrates concedes that his contradictory manner (ἀντιλογικῶς) evinces his combativeness (ἀγωνισταὶ) (164c8–d2; see *Sophist* 231d12–e2, 232b1–7). It is this, Socrates' self-rebuke, that prepares for Protagoras' second, longer, and more robust self-defense.

Protagoras immediately returns the favor of Socrates' attack with a two-part defense that addresses each of Socrates' arguments in turn, and then closes by challenging him to live up to the standard of argumentation philosophy sets for itself. It is to Protagoras' credit, and likewise Socrates' discredit, that Protagoras' methodology, if you will, is superior to the method implicit in Socrates' behavior.[6] Protagoras justly takes Socrates to task, as he advances a

---

[6] If Euclides hadn't removed Socrates' comments on the dialogue, perhaps at this point Socrates would have confessed that he blushed, though the more likely candidate is in the vicinity of 196d1–3. Socrates' gingerly treatment of Theaetetus guarantees that the youth did not blush. As for Theodorus, one can think of moments where he might have grown red with anger and which Socrates may have portrayed as a blush (consider 169a6–b4, *Republic* 350c12–d3).

more coherent version of his account that exposes the shortsightedness of his Athenian adversary (see 166a2–b2, c2–d1, 167d4–168c2). Protagoras first rebuts the memory argument by arguing that, in a world in flux, there is no room for sameness, such that it would be possible, per Socrates' example, for someone to perceive something, then close his eyes (and thus not perceive and know it), while remembering (and thus knowing) that same thing. Not only are what he perceived and what he remembers necessarily different, so too is *he*—indeed, he is becoming limitless (166b2–c2; see 154a6–9). Protagoras thus concludes that it is not he himself but Socrates who is the swine (166c7: ὗς). He then rebuts the expertise argument by basing expertise on the distinction between good and bad rather than true and false: the expert does not change one's opinion or experience from false to true but from worse to better, that is, he produces what appears and thus is good (166d5–167d4; compare *Protagoras* 318a1–9). Like his modern counterparts, Protagoras makes the good a matter of individual fancy. Upon making this second counterpoint, Protagoras concludes with a long exhortation to justice in questioning, that is, an exhortation to discerning the difference between competing (ἀγωνιζόμενος) and conversing (διαλεγόμενος); only by attending to the latter, Protagoras warns, will Socrates have any chance of making his interlocutor (τὸν προσδιαλεγόμενον) turn to philosophy, rather than having those Socrates is with (τοὺς συνόντας) hate his activity or business (τὸ πρᾶγμα) (167d4–168c2; compare *Apology of Socrates* 20c4–d1, 23a7–b4, *Crito* 53c7–d1). The power of Protagoras' response—in coupling rigorous defense with approbation and exhortation—induces in Theodorus an admiration for the youthful liveliness (νεανικῶς) of Socrates' assistance (168c6–7). To his mind, Socrates has put himself in his place. This self-critique, coupled with Socrates' insistent goading of the reluctant Theodorus to enter the conversation, both here and elsewhere, plants and even nurtures the seed of Theodorus' criticism of Socrates at the start of the *Sophist*.

Though Protagoras responded to both of Socrates' attacks, Socrates develops only the expertise argument. It is humorous that

Socrates' omission will lead him to celebrate the comprehensiveness of the philosopher's vision—rather, it is ominous, as this omission will prove essential to his downfall in Act Two. He begins by pitting experts and non-experts against one another, arguing that in Protagoras' case the many will opine that Protagoras opines falsely, so that if, per Protagoras' argument, their opinions are true, then Protagoras' work, *The Truth*, is false (169d3–171c7). Socrates' argument requires that he drop the dative, that is, that he obscure the point that these opinions about Protagoras' work would be true only *for* those who opine them.[7] Nevertheless, Socrates draws some conclusions from this argument that attempt to locate the cause of Protagoras' error, namely, as regards the difference between the opinions of experts like Protagoras and those of his many detractors. In the case of sciences like medicine, experts are readily acknowledged (171d9–e9). But in the case of politics, no layman or city is in any way wiser regarding the holy and unholy, just and unjust, or beautiful and shameful (172a1–8). Rather, in such cases, "they want to insist (ἰσχυρίζεσθαι) that none of these [terms] is by nature in possession of its own being (οὐσίαν)," that is, that in these cases Protagorean relativism holds true (172b1–6). Socrates thus argues that Protagoras has made the error of overextending a commonplace, rather naïve critique of convention so as to encompass all of science (ἐπιστήμη) and expertise (σοφία).[8] Socrates makes one exception among the categories invoked in political discourse—namely, the advantageous—which would appear to have a higher ontological status than the others mentioned (172a8–b2).[9] We expect Socrates

---

[7] See Burnyeat 1990, 29. One wonders whether the drop of the dative may rather foreshadow the coming argument that rescues objectivity from Protagorean relativism.

[8] See note 10.

[9] More precisely, Socrates drops the beautiful and the shameful from his second list, an omission that implies they have a higher ontological status than the just and unjust and the holy and unholy but a lower one than the advantageous. The reasons for this will become apparent in Chapter IV, Section IV.

to explain this higher ontological status immediately. He will eventually do so, but only after he indulges himself by going on a long digression celebrating philosophic freedom. Socrates senses that he is on the cusp of showing a link between the good and the true that would demolish Protagoras' defense of his expertise as concerned with the good in abstraction from the true. He can therefore hardly contain himself (172b8–c2) from praising the extraordinary freedom and leisure that philosophers enjoy (172c8–d5, 175d7–e1) and that grant them a cosmically large vision that easily exposes at a mere glance the petty smallness of all the bickering and boasting of those embroiled in the city's more immediate concerns (174b9–175b7). Most relevantly, this freedom and leisure give philosophers ample time to speak so as to happen upon being or what is (τὸ ὄν), so that they escape the narrow confines of urgency in courts and political affairs (172d8–173b2). That is to say, having just pages ago been reproached by Protagoras for his shortsightedness, Socrates now celebrates the extent and grandeur of the philosopher's vision in distinction from the sophisticated but still sloppy solipsism and (we may now say) conventionalism of his adversary—a distinction founded on the distance between seeming and being.[10] This grand vision of philosophic freedom is much more to Theodorus' mind than Socrates' actual behavior had been and, indeed, will be (see 175e1 with 176a2–4).

When Socrates returns from his digression, he is slow to hold himself to this distinction and nearly stops too soon. His argument concludes in two stages. In the first, he returns to the point from which he had digressed: though an opinion about the just is not necessarily shaken by bad consequences, the same cannot be said of the good once its consequences have been reaped; for, when the good an opinion promises does not obtain, no one can avoid calling that opinion false in retrospect (177c6–179a9). Thus, the true and

---

[10] On the various forms of conventionalism, see Strauss 1953, 10–12, 93–117. See, also, Priou 2018c.

the good, which Protagoras attempted to keep separate so as to reconcile his relativism with his claim to expertise, Socrates now shows to be inseparable. What we mean by the good is the *truly* good, not the apparent good: an apparent good that does not deliver on its promises is no good at all but something of a beautiful fiction. As he rounds out his response to Protagoras' rebuttal, Socrates grows quite confident in his conclusions (178e9: Νὴ Δία) but pulls back suddenly at the very end (179c5). As he immediately confesses, he has failed to live up to Protagoras' exhortation and so must examine the sophist's hypothesis more closely by looking at its ontological underpinnings (179c5–d4). But by neglecting to look to Protagoras' ontology in particular, he has failed to meet not only Protagoras' standard for philosophic inquiry but his own as well. For in the digression Socrates exalted the free and leisurely philosopher for taking the time necessary to tailor his speeches to being rather than succumbing to fleeting exigencies, while it is precisely the fleeting exigency of dismissing Protagoras' hypothesis to which Socrates now confesses he has succumbed. And even though when Socrates does consider Protagoras' ontology the results are rather devastating for his hypothesis, nevertheless there will again be an omission. For while he initially intends to discuss both the fluxists and the monists, Socrates ultimately treats only the fluxists—this suffices, it turns out, to dismiss Protagoras' hypothesis (see 181a4–b7, 183b7–d2). Just as with the omission of the memory argument, then, so too will our hero be haunted in Act Two by his omission of the monists—specifically of Parmenides, before whom Socrates withdraws in reverential shame (183e3–184a2, esp. 183e6–7: αἰδοῖός τέ μοι...δεινός τε). Thus, despite his efforts, Socrates' omissions will betray that he has not held himself to his own standard of comprehensiveness. That standard rather aids Theodorus in generating his later criticism of Socrates at the beginning of the *Sophist*.

Socrates' final, most fundamental, but nevertheless only partial attack on Protagoras' hypothesis considers the possibility of meaningful speech for a fluxist ontology. In a world where everything moves by every kind of motion, nothing remains the same; but if nothing remains the same, then what one speaks of now is not the same at the next moment, so that the perception or knowledge of which he speaks necessarily becomes non-perception or non-knowledge, that is, something other than that of which he spoke before (182c3–183b2). Consequently, the fluxists "don't have any expressions (ῥήματα) for their hypothesis" (183b3–4). The relativist hypothesis cannot even rise to the dignity of being an hypothesis. What the fluxists fail to grasp, therefore, is that we do not perceive the world by means of the organs of perception, but rather our various perceptions travel *through* them and together into some one look or form (μίαν τινὰ ἰδέαν) called the soul (184b4–185e2). Thus, not the body but the soul, when it is by itself, troubles itself with being and the good (185e3–186b1). That is, though certain things are present by nature for us to perceive as experiences, still when (per the expertise argument) we consider the good in a future time we necessarily touch upon truth and therewith being (186b11–c8). Thus, Protagoras' expertise—indeed, all expertise and science—does not concern experience and perception but being and truth (186c9–e12).[11]

Knowledge, therefore, is not perception but rather a gathering-up (ἀναλογισμός) or gathering-together (συλλογισμός) about (πρός) our perceptions (186b11–c5, d2–5). It is there that Socrates and Theaetetus must look, and immediately will look, if they are to find knowledge. Having demonstrated the possibility—but *only* the possibility—of expertise and, further, that expertise is impossible without a distinction between true and false, Socrates has chased away Protagoras' ghost and so completed his exorcism of Theaetetus. But thus far the process has been only negative. As Socrates says, it was not to find what knowledge is not, but what it is, that they began conversing (187a1–3). Will Socrates and Theaetetus indeed figure out what knowledge is? Will this discovery help them

---

[11] Socrates' argument would only make sense, it seems, if the good is beyond being and the cause of being, that is, only if the position advanced in *Republic* VII is correct.

bury the newly slain Protagoras as a mere aberration of the intellect? Or will Protagoras succeed in repossessing Theaetetus' soul and getting his vengeance on Socrates? For all this, we must see whether they succeed in their attempt to find something *beyond* perception, some gathering-up or gathering-together of our perceptions, that we can, with the demonstrative force of a geometric proof, call knowledge of the truth of the beings.

III.

We turn, then, to Act Two, which like Act One comprises two scenes. In Scene One, Socrates considers Theaetetus' first proposal for where to look for knowledge beyond perception: opinion—specifically, true opinion (187a1–b8). Theaetetus' answer raises for Socrates an old question regarding the possibility of opining falsely (187c7–d6), and it is in this discussion that the bottom drops out from the dialogue as a whole. For, as Socrates remarks, someone might rebuke them for implicitly claiming all along that they know the things they've been agreeing to, despite not knowing what knowledge even is (192d12–e7). That is, the attempt to distinguish opinions into true and false relies on their having already been so distinguished, inasmuch as every statement uttered in that attempt purports to be a true opinion. Behind knowledge as true opinion lurks man, the measure of all things. Facing this revival of Protagorean relativism, Socrates and Theaetetus consider in Scene Two what has since become the canonical definition of knowledge: justified true belief—or, as Socrates and Theaetetus put it, a true opinion with an account (λόγος) (201c7–d3).[12] In his consideration of what

---

[12] Famously, Gettier showed the incompleteness of this formulation by pointing out how a weak understanding of "justified" allows for certain justified true beliefs to qualify as knowledge, despite not being knowledge (see Gettier 1976). Gettier points to the *Theaetetus* (and *Meno*) as having versions of this formulation, citing in addition the views of Ayer 1956 and Chisholm 1957. Though in the *Theaetetus* they are concerned with knowledge of univer-

this account adds to a true opinion, so that it becomes knowledge, Socrates presents the account as binding that opinion to being—either by going through a being's parts or by indicating its difference from all else that is. But the result is either solipsism, and thus a return to Protagorean relativism, or redundancy, and thus no improvement over the previous definition. Socrates' victory in Act One is thus shown to be spurious, as Protagoras once again assumes the helm of Theaetetus' soul. After this tragic denouement to Socrates' attempt to affirm the possibility and necessity of philosophy, we will turn in Section IV to the dialogue's brief and somber epilogue.

As soon as Theaetetus proposes that knowledge is *true* opinion, Socrates is drawn into a consideration of *false* opinion. Indeed, he appears altogether consumed by it: his attempts to understand false opinion occupy nearly the whole discussion of Theaetetus' second definition, with his actual refutation taking less than a page of the discussion's fourteen (compare 187c7–200d4 with 200d5–201c6). This digression will expose the repercussions of Socrates' omissions from his argument in Act One, that is, Protagoras' response to the memory argument and, especially, the thought of Parmenides.[13] Indulging in Theaetetus' offer to take full advantage of their aforementioned leisure (187d9–11), Socrates proposes five accounts of false opinion, the first three logical and the last two analogical. Socrates works through the logical accounts rather quickly. He proposes first that one opines falsely either when one opines something one knows to be something else one knows, in which case one does not actually know those things; or that it occurs when one opines something one does not know as something else one does not know,

---

sals and not particulars, per Gettier's examples, still Gettier discerns that justification's everyday and philosophic senses are less clearly determined than one supposes. Socrates himself suggests as much by pointing to the connection between law-courts and mathematical proofs. See the discussion of Act Two, Scene Two in Section III, paragraphs 9 through 14.

[13] Benardete 1984, I.147 goes so far as to give the title "Parmenides" to the section of his commentary treating the three logical solutions to the problem of false opinion. Compare Cropsey 1995, 52.

though one would have to know what one does not know in order to confuse them (187e5–188c9). Dissatisfied, Socrates proposes in the second place that one opines falsely whenever one opines the things that are not, that is, the non-beings (τὰ μὴ ὄντα) (188c10–d6). But just as to see or to hear is always to see or to hear something, so, too, to opine must always be to opine something (and not nothing) (188d7–189b9). The third and final logical proposal has the one who opines falsely opining one thing (τὸ ἕτερον) as another (ἕτερον) (189b10–c7). But since it is altogether unfathomable, for example, to think of someone opining the odd as even or two as one, this definition also won't do (189c8–190d11, esp. 190c4: Μὰ Δί[α]). All three definitions rest on the assumption that, concerning everything and with respect to each individually, one either knows or doesn't know them (188a1–2). Our discussion of this assumption is best saved for when we return to the *Theaetetus* in Chapter Four. For at present, again, we are concerned only with Theaetetus' and Theodorus' unplayful, all-too-serious understanding of the conversation, and Socrates' present interlocutor Theaetetus deems this assumption reasonable. Thus, the salient point at present is that, despite his efforts, Socrates' attempts at a logical understanding of false opinion have failed, and so have not met the geometer's standard of demonstration, advanced by Protagoras and likewise accepted and later recalled by Socrates (162e5–163a1, 163a2, 179d2–3). And so, as he prepares to shift from the logical to the analogical—analogical and so, we might now say, an image and false (see 150a8–b2, b9–c3, e6–7, 151c2–4, d2–3)—Socrates fears shame at being stuck in such perplexity (190e8–191a1). The one consolation Socrates sees is that, should he and Theaetetus succeed in escaping this perplexity, they will subsequently look upon all others as perplexed; nevertheless, should they not, then they will be all the worse off for it (191a1–6). For the first time, Socrates sees himself starting to run out of options.

This dramatic touch upon Socrates' shift from the logical solutions to the analogical is the first and slightest of the moments tracking Socrates' tragic fall. The next occurs after the first analogical

Theaetetus

solution brings them face-to-face with the problem of false opinion. Socrates returns to the assumption of the logical solutions, according to which we either know or don't know everything, excluding all learning and forgetting (191a8–b1; see 188a1–6). He now wants to understand the possibility of knowing something in terms of degrees, as a process or genesis (191c3–7). So, for the sake of argument (δή...λόγου ἕνεκα), he has Theaetetus posit that we have in our souls a lump of wax, upon which impressions are made by our perceptions and thoughts (αἰσθήσεσι καὶ ἐννοίαις) (191c8–d8). Socrates articulates at great length and in excruciating detail the relationship between perception and memory (191e3–194b7, esp. 192c7–8 and d2). He ultimately identifies cases of false opinion as occurring when one is cognizant of or familiar with (γιγνώσκειν) two things but perceives both or just one at a distance, so that one easily confuses the perception with the impression on the wax block, as though a paltry archer (τοξότην φαῦλον) (193e6–194a8). We have in Socrates' mixing of metaphors a small indication of why he was forced to employ an analogical rather than logical solution. Recall that, at the end of Socrates' refutation of the first definition of knowledge, he distinguished between the things that exist by nature for us and for any animal to perceive, on the one hand, and the gathering-up and gathering-together of these things, wherein being and truth are purported to lie, on the other (186b11–c6). This distinction led them, in turn, to search for knowledge in that gathering-up and gathering-together—as they understand it in the second definition, when the process of thinking culminates in a true opinion and when in a false one. Socrates' three logical solutions looked at these intellectual operations only in a static way, as completed such that one is opining falsely. But what Socrates seeks and now attempts to describe is the *genesis* of a false opinion, the process or activity by which it comes into being, how it is that the gathering-up and gathering-together might go awry. The essential difficulty is that, when we are in the process of coming to opine falsely, we appear both to know and not to know the same thing, while also not quite doing either of the two (187e5–188c9). One is a poor archer, skillful but not free from error. Socrates must therefore expand the quick and simple task of pressing a signet ring into a lump of wax into the more challenging task of hitting a target at a much greater distance. Only with such a gap between the act of perception and the formation of an opinion does the analogy make false opinion somewhat comprehensible. But when Socrates next considers the adequacy of his image (195b6–7), it becomes immediately clear that he hasn't actually described an error in an intellectual process but rather an error in applying a weak perception to something one already knows (195c6–d3). That is, though he began with perceptions *and* thoughts, his account so far has concerned only perceptions imprinted upon our memory. He has not, therefore, accounted for such purely intellectual errors as we encounter, for example, in mathematical calculations, whenever one confuses two numbers one knows (195d6–196c8). How could one ever arrive at a false opinion about the things one knows when treating them solely as knowledge, that is, on a wholly intellectual and non-perceptual level? With this question, Socrates is plunged into the second moment of despair in his tragic denouement, as he discerns some stirrings of life in Protagoras' corpse.

Why this question would give Socrates cause for concern immediately becomes apparent when we join Socrates in considering "that from the beginning our entire speech or argument (λόγος) has come to be a searching (ζήτησις) for knowledge" (196d8–9), that is, that their whole activity has been a meditation on intellectual processes, that they have been thinking about thinking (189e4–190a6). Considering that they don't know what knowledge is, they have for a long time been "filled up with impure conversing" (ἀνάπλεῳ τοῦ μὴ καθαρῶς διαλέγεσθαι) (196d11–e2). The impurity consists in their implicit claim with every assertion that they know what they assert, which in turn relies on an assumption about the nature of knowledge (196e2–7). Knowledge of knowledge is necessary, it would seem, before we are to seek knowledge of anything. The question, What is knowledge?, *qua* question exposes the difficulty, if not impossibility, of an altogether pure foundation to our knowledge.

Socrates' celebration of philosophers as occupying a place purified of evils (177a5: ὁ τῶν κακῶν καθαρὸς τόπος) was the dream of a necessarily impure soul, and as such a dream it was, like every agreement they have made, merely a product of circumstances. Behind Socratic searching (ζήτησις) lies man, the measure of all things, for whom all he asserts appears and thus is true. Socrates imagines an anonymous, manly contradictor taking him and Theaetetus to task for the impurity of their speech (197a1–3). We suspect, of course, that this manly contradictor is Protagoras, who would have shown by such an argument that his relativism infects not only our sensory perceptions but our opinions, as well. Such was indeed suggested by the ease with which both Socrates and Theaetetus spoke of the activity of soul that makes clear (185c5: δηλοῖ) truth and being as both thinking and perceiving (185a4–6: περὶ ἀμφοτέρων διανοῇ...περὶ ἀμφοτέρων αἰσθάνοι' ἄν; see 185b7: διανοῇ, also 185e2: ἐπισκοπεῖν, 186a4–5: ἐπορέγεται, a11: σκοπεῖσθαι).[14] The gulf Socrates established between appearance and being,[15] between convention and nature, and so between the city and the philosopher is not so great as he had presumed. Socrates' life of leisure did not grant him the freedom he so celebrated.

This moment thus exposes a long-standing Socratic hubris, one going back to the beginning of the dialogue. But it goes back still earlier, to the first Socratic conversation Plato depicts. For when Socrates encountered Parmenides as a youth, the aged Eleatic warned him that the greatest impasse facing the power of dialectics is the skeptic who denies human beings access to or the existence of precise knowledge, that is, knowledge precise in the sense of one (*Parmenides* 133a8–c1, 134c4–e8). And now, late in life, Socrates encounters the skeptic who explicitly avers that nothing is one in

---

[14] As is well known, the original sense of νοεῖν was that of perceiving acutely. For the benchmark studies, see von Fritz 1943 and 1945, Lesher 1981 and 1994.

[15] Consider, too, that Socrates' argument against his second logical definition of false opinion relied on the assumption that opining is similar to the various modes of perception (188e4–189a5).

itself, only to have shown himself not up to the task Parmenides bequeathed him in his youth, that of instructing the skeptic in his errors (*Parmenides* 134e9–135b4).[16] Socrates thus satisfies neither Parmenides nor the sophist, a fact reflected in the first of his two most glaring omissions from the argument of Act One, namely, his failure to address Protagoras' response to the memory argument. According to that response, our memories and, indeed, we ourselves are always changing from moment to moment: everyone's lump of wax is more fluid than firm (194e1–195a4). In Act One, Scene One, this flux meant that knowledge is perception. But Socrates' argument in Scene Two still stands: truth and being are not to be sought in our perceptions but in the gathering-up or gathering-together of our perceptions, in relation to what does not change in us, our abiding love of the good. Now, however, we see that the two arguments suggest that, though knowledge is to be *sought* in the gathering up and gathering together of our perceptions, it is tragically never to be found. As has been observed, Socrates conflated perception and appearance in his discussion of the first definition by reducing the latter to the former.[17] Appearance, that ambiguous realm between the perception of things and knowledge of the beings, offers Protagoras a refuge, from which he can make his rejoinder to Socrates in the guise of the anonymous, manly contradictor.

Protagoras is further aided by Socrates' second glaring omission, namely, the thought of the monists and, specifically, the "revered and uncanny" Parmenides (183e6–7: αἰδοῖός τέ...δεινός τε). For in his poem Parmenides encounters a goddess who argues that being is one and has no room for non-being, a revelation that leads her to conclude that the mixing of being and non-being in human speech of necessity confines human beings to ineluctable error (Parmenides B8.50–53, B19).[18] Though this conclusion is op-

---

[16] For my fuller discussion, see Priou 2018a, 47–73.
[17] See Burnyeat 1990, 21.
[18] See note 9 to the Overture.

posed to Protagoras' claim that all opinions are true, still the goddess' denigration of the limits of human capacities offers Protagoras a rejoinder to Socrates' critique that preserves his fluxist account of the human world (Parmenides B8.50–52). In short, the instability of the human soul, of which Protagoras spoke in his response to the memory argument, finds deeper expression in the goddess' judgment of man as a two-headed wanderer (Parmenides B6). It is this possibility that emerges in the figure of the anonymous contradictor. Thus, in Act One Protagoras was the skeptic who denied that anything is one in itself, while in Act Two he becomes the skeptic who denies us access to the one that is, asserting instead an unbridgeable separation between appearance and being. Parmenides himself had warned Socrates of this other possibility (*Parmenides* 135a3–5). Wielding the sword of Parmenidean logic, Protagoras lands a blow on Socrates.[19] Socrates has made Protagoras young and beautiful. And such will he remain until the Eleatic Stranger exhibits the courage to attack the argument of his philosophical father Parmenides and in so doing make possible an account of false opinion.

To return to the argument, the image of the memory as a lump of wax in our souls could not account for purely intellectual errors, which defect in turn brought to Socrates' attention the applicability of this argument to his own activity. Admitting that they have implicitly assumed that they know what knowledge is and that this unproven assumption exposes them as paltry (φαῦλοι), Socrates dares (τολμήσω) to say what is meant by the verb "to know" (τὸ ἐπίστασθαι) (197a3–6; compare 173c8–9). Whereas what is presently meant by knowing is a having or holding of knowledge (ἐπιστήμης...ἕξιν), Socrates proposes that they instead understand it as a possession of knowledge (ἐπιστήμης κτῆσιν) (197a7–b4). By possession, Socrates means something that one has acquired (τὸ κεκτῆσθαι) but isn't presently holding (τὸ ἔχειν) (197b5–13).

---

[19] Like the present reading of the *Theaetetus*, so too the present reading of Parmenides' poem must lack playfulness. For my more playful thoughts on Parmenides, see Priou 2018b.

What motivates Socrates to introduce this distinction is the need to create the same gap within the activity of thought as there was between perception and memory in the wax image: only with such a gap is the image of the archer applicable to such purely intellectual errors as Theaetetus has experienced while studying mathematics. Socrates thus revises his image of the soul as a lump of wax to that of the soul as a dovecote, in which one possesses the things that he knows and that he must hunt in order to hold or have them (197c1–e1). The dovecote image explains the genesis of a false opinion—say, that the sum of seven and four is twelve—as follows: when attempting to "seize"—or whatever we call it (198a1–4, 198e1–199a6)[20]—the knowledge of eleven one possesses, one hunts for it among all the fluttering birds of knowledge in his dovecote; then seizes, instead of the knowledge of eleven sought, the knowledge of twelve as they fly about one another; and thus opines falsely that the sum of seven and four is twelve (199a6–b7). Conversely, when one seizes the right knowledge-bird, one possesses a true opinion as knowledge (199b8–c4). The archer's arrow thus becomes the reaching hand, with the earlier gap between perception and knowledge effectively introduced within thinking itself.

In so solving the problem of false opinion, Socrates and Theaetetus appear to have escaped the shamefulness of the way they've been conducting the argument (λόγος). But the reprieve from laughter is short-lived, as Protagoras returns—again, anonymously—to disenchant Socrates with his solution. Upon arriving at his solution, Socrates wastes no time in pointing out that the image implies one is ignorant by means of knowledge, as though one is blind by means of sight (199d1–8). That is, how can one make a mistake by seizing upon knowledge? Theaetetus attempts to plug this leaky ship by proposing that the dovecote contain not just knowledge but non-knowledge, as well; but Socrates points out that

---

[20] Socrates avoids speaking of ἀνάμνησις, that is, of the myth of learning as recollection as found in the *Meno* and *Phaedo*. For a discussion of his avoidance, see Klein 1965, 158–66 and Stern 2008, 221–22.

the refuter from before (ὁ...ἐλεγκτικὸς ἐκεῖνος)—that is, the anonymous, new, and more beautiful Protagoras—would laugh at them while going through a laundry list of difficulties about knowing both knowledge and non-knowledge, mistaking non-knowledge for what one knows, and so on—difficulties unfathomably insurmountable to Theaetetus (199e1–200c6, esp. c5: Ἀλλὰ μὰ Δί[α]). That refuter, who threatened to throw Socrates and Theaetetus into shameful perplexity, now returns to rob them of their last understanding of false opinion. And in so doing, he confines them once again to the inescapable particularity and privacy of their perceptions and opinions. Having trembled as he switched from his logical to analogical solutions, then felt shame at the entirety of his conduct even to his earliest days, Socrates now faces the insurmountable problem of demonstrating the veracity or falsity of an opinion. And so he asks Theaetetus, once again, what knowledge is (200d5–9). Socrates' treatment of the final definition will show him how he has long lived in a somnolescent state, as a diseased and dreaming philosopher who fancies himself traversing the cosmos high above the city, though he stands in Athens' streets, dawdling in her schools. At least, that is how a Theodorus would receive it.

Act Two, Scene Two exposes Socrates' dream as follows. Upon hearing Socrates once again pose the question, What is knowledge?, Theaetetus requests that they reconsider his most recent definition, true opinion, as the digression on false opinion has done nothing to indict the infallibility (ἀναμάρτητόν γέ) of true opinion, that is, its reliability in practical affairs (200d5–e6).[21] Socrates' counterexample decisively refutes Theaetetus' second definition, while at the same time pointing to a standard for knowledge that prompts Theaetetus to give us his third and final definition. In political affairs, it is common for rhetors and lawyers to persuade and thus produce opinions

---

[21] As Benardete shows, however, the failure to define false opinion is a failure to define true opinion: "Socrates' digression on false opinion is not a digression at all, but rather an account of what is involved in the soul's pronouncement on its own phantom image, 'True'" (Benardete 2000, 316).

in their audiences, but in a span of time that isn't sufficient for teaching and thus making them know (201a3–b7). In court cases, especially, there are certainly instances where a juror arrives at a correct opinion that doesn't appear to be knowledge (201b8–c6). Socrates here invokes an image from his digression on the freedom and leisure of the philosopher, namely, the image of the political man with a soul warped like wet wood from the water-clock constraining his speech (172c8–173b3). Such a man lacks the leisure to tailor his speeches to being. Refuted thus by Socrates' argument and also moved by his own recollection of Socrates' depiction of the free philosopher, Theaetetus responds with his third and final definition of knowledge, one he has heard but whose source he has now forgotten: knowledge is true opinion with an account (μετὰ λόγου); that is, the knower can supplement his true opinion with what the juror's haste, and non-perception of the crime, prevent him from finding but the philosopher has ample time to seek out: reason (λόγος) (201c7–d2). It is not difficult to see from where Theaetetus may have heard this definition. It takes the form of such geometer's proofs as we find in Euclid's *Elements*, to which Theaetetus would become an eventual contributor: a true opinion is announced—"I say that *x*"—and then followed by a demonstration—the aforementioned account (λόγος). In his freedom from the confines of the courtroom's perversions, the high-flying philosopher rips speech (λόγος) from the world of petty politics and tailors it to the majesty of being, tethering his true opinions to reality with the geometer's rigorous demonstrations and so transforming them into knowledge. Such is their dream.

Thus, in Act Two, Scene Two—the final bit of drama before the dialogue's brief epilogue (Section IV)—Socrates tests Theaetetus' third definition, and in so doing puts on trial his own torpid vision of the philosopher's freedom and leisure (see 208b12–c1, esp. κατηγορῶμεν). Socrates makes a distinction between the intelligible things (τὰ ἐπιστητά) and the unintelligible things (τὰ μὴ ἐπιστητά), that is, being is such that in certain cases to be also means to be knowable (201d2–5). Socrates elaborates on Theaetetus' vague recollection with what he calls a dream, according to which the ultimate elements (στοιχεῖα) of things are so simple as to be unintelligible and only nameable; only the compounds (τὰ...συγκείμενα) woven from these elements can be spoken, when we likewise weave their names together into a speech (λόγος) (201d6–202b8). In cases where we lack this speech, we opine truly but do not have knowledge; but when we do have it we are perfect in point of knowledge (τελείως πρὸς ἐπιστήμην ἔχειν) (202b8–c6). With these premises in place, Socrates outlines what we will call both here and in subsequent chapters *the dilemma of intelligibility*. The dilemma runs as follows. A compound is either all the elements or some one look that comes into being when they are set together (203c4–7).[22] Assuming it is all the elements, he who knows each of two elements is agreed to know both; but it is uncanny and startling (δεινὸν, ἐξαίφνης)[23] to think that someone can know both elements while knowing neither of the two (203c8–e1). Thus, the compound isn't all the elements. They consider next, therefore, that it is some one look (ἰδέα) that comes into being when all the elements are set together (203e2–204a4). This brings them to the following question. How do we mean "look" (ἰδέα)? Is it a whole of parts, or is it indivisibly one? If it is a whole of parts, then the whole is either all the parts—so that the compound would, again, be all the elements and thus unknowable—or some look (εἶδος) other than all its parts (204a5–10). But it is agreed that, just as with "four plus two" or "three plus three" the whole "six" is all the elements, so too is any whole all its parts (204a11–205a7). Thus, again the whole is all the

---

[22] Socrates also proposes it may be both, if there are only two, but in the subsequent argument he takes this case to be no different than if it were all the elements. This assumption is of course specious, as ἀμφότερα implies, both in its meaning and in its comparative root -ερ-, that two things together have some one look different from each one that the look comprises; thus two possesses a quality that each unit lacks: it is even. Compare Priou 2018a, 102.

[23] On the connection between the sudden and startling, see Daube 1964, 1–2.

elements and, again, unknowable (205a8–b13). The only remaining option is that the compound is "some one, indivisible look" (μία τις ἰδέα ἀμέριστος) (205c1–3). But that just makes the compound as one as each of the elements, and so again unknowable (205c4–e5). Whence the startling and dream-disrupting dilemma of intelligibility: nothing, it turns out, can be known.

Of course, it isn't difficult to see that the preceding argument relies on the unproven assumption that, with respect to each thing, the entire number (ὁ...ἀριθμὸς πᾶς) is the entire being (τὸ ὂν πᾶν) (204d10–11). Tempting though it may be to critique this assumption now, we must hold off until Chapter Four. For we are, again, engaged in a decidedly unplayful reading, one befitting the seriousness of Theaetetus and Theodorus, for whom mathematics provides *the* model for knowledge and so numbers *the* model for the beings (see 146c7–d3). And as *they* perceive it, the argument has run into an insoluble dilemma. Nevertheless, Socrates immediately finds a way out by turning to Theaetetus' experience of what he has learned—letters, lyre-playing, and (by extension) that initial list of arts he claimed to have learned from Theodorus and which he offered up as a "definition" of knowledge (206a1–b4). What this experience shows Theaetetus is that, far from being unintelligible, the elements (or letters) are *more* intelligible than the syllables, with exceptionally large aggregates proving especially difficult to understand (206b5–12). The dilemma of intelligibility has thus led them to retreat into an understanding of being familiar to these mathematicians—into what we will later term *the ontology of method*.[24] That is, it has not so much shown them that nothing can be known, as it has reinforced for them the futility of searching for a science beyond those employing or able to employ mathematics. And though Socrates will continue his efforts, still the results will bring him back to Protagorean relativism—to a solipsism Socrates' vanity has cloaked from his view. Protagoras nudges the sleepy Socrates.

---

[24] Compare Descartes' account of the difficulty in imagining a chiliagon in *Meditations on First Philosophy* Meditation 6.

Theaetetus

The nudging soon turns to shaking. Having seen that knowledge isn't possible given the unintelligibility of the elements, Socrates considers whether the mathematician's position that they are rather intelligible—and more so than the compounds—would make tenable the definition of knowledge as a true opinion with an account. Since they seek to show that both the elements and their compounds are intelligible, Socrates and Theaetetus agree that adding an account (λόγος) to a true opinion would give one the most complete or perfect knowledge (τὴν τελεωτάτην ἐπιστήμην) (206c1–6). Socrates proposes three understandings of an account in this context. The first is making one's own thought apparent through sound with verbs and nouns (206d1–2). This is, however, the bare minimum one could expect of *any* speech, and so it immediately appears that nearly everyone is capable of doing or making this (πᾶς ποιεῖν δυνατὸς) (206d7–8). Socrates represents such an account streaming from one's mouth as a reflection of a thought in a mirror or water, as though a private opinion deemed true by its holder. The imagery of rivers and mirrors in this proposal illustrates that it implies a Protagorean world of flux and relativism. The aim of the next two proposals will thus be to escape this vain self-reflection (compare 208c5 with 150b1, c2, e7, 151c3: εἴδωλον; see, also, Heraclitus B17). Socrates' second proposal is that they search for one who is "capable (δυνατὸν), when asked what each thing is, to give back an answer through the elements to him who is asking" (206e6–207a1). This second understanding of an account doesn't succeed because it is conceivable that one can go through the elements while not knowing them. To use Socrates' example, one who knows how to spell the name ΘΕΑΙΤΗΤΟΣ (Theaetetus) knows that it begins ΘΕ (The); but knowing this, he could still also erroneously spell ΘΕΟΔΟΡΟΣ (Theodorus) by beginning with ΤΕ (Te); thus he would know how to spell ΘΕΑΙΤΗΤΟΣ (Theaetetus) by going through the elements, while not knowing those elements themselves (207a2–208b10). We note in passing that, in accordance with the preceding, this is an exceedingly arithmetical understanding of letters, according to which the "units" that comprise a word do not differ depending on the word in which they are found, that is, on the whole. Questionable though this may be, the argument meets with the young mathematician's approval, so that Socrates' second understanding of what speech adds to true opinion fails. Noticing this failure to escape the solipsism of the first proposal, Socrates jumps to the conclusion that he's been awoken from his dream—that his hope to tailor in leisure his speech to being has been dashed (208b11–12).

Immediately following this moment of wakeful clarity, Socrates quickly recalls that he had mentioned a third and final understanding of an account, and so dozes off again (208b12–c6). It is on this point that Scene Two draws to a close and Act Two with it. Socrates proposes that he who has added an account to his true opinion "is able to say some sign by which the thing asked about differs from all things" (208c7–8). After some explication for Theaetetus' sake, Socrates again becomes disenchanted, saying that he now doesn't comprehend even a little, since he is close (ἐγγὺς) to what is being said just as a shadow painting (σκιαγραφήματος); for, so long as he stood away from it (ἀφειστήκη) from afar (πόρρωθεν), it appeared to him to make sense (τί...λέγεσθαι) (208e7–10). The language of Socrates' brief comment here refers subtly back to his youthful conversation with Parmenides. At one point during Parmenides' lengthy examination of the being and non-being of unity, the elder Eleatic investigated the consequences for human experience should there be no unity in being—that is, he articulated the position of the skeptic, of whom Parmenides warned Socrates earlier in their conversation and whose later ilk would include Protagoras. Parmenides argued there that, when seen from afar (πόρρωθεν), a heap of things will necessarily appear to be one; but, when thought sharply from up close (ἐγγύθεν), each one thing will reveal itself to be limitless in multitude; consequently, these heaps appear to have experienced the same thing and to be like, just like shadow paintings (ἐσκιαγραφημένα) that appear one to somebody standing away from them (ἀποστάντι) (*Parmenides* 165b7–d1).[25] Socrates' allusion to his conversation in the *Parmenides* is pregnant with significance, for it is here that Parmenides considers Protagoras' thesis: everything only appears to be one to him looking, while nothing actually is one in its being. Thus, at this moment in the *Theaetetus*, Socrates sees himself trapped in Protagoras' world, at one moment dreamily believing himself to have sure possession of knowledge, only later to realize upon waking that his knowledge, when viewed from up close, is but an incoherent patchwork.

Socrates' reference to shadow paintings also recalls the *Republic*'s famous image of cave dwellers bound in their subterranean prison and deceived that shadow paintings cast upon the wall by the false light of fire are the things themselves, a condition from which the philosopher flees, making his way up and out to the natural light of the sun (*Republic* 514a ff.). This escape, Socrates says, is almost—though not exactly—like putting sight into blind eyes (*Republic* 518b7–519b6; but compare 506c6–10). But now, in the *Theaetetus*, just as Socrates anticipates losing his last chance at escape,[26] he imagines himself deceived by shadow paintings and like a blind man trapped in inescapable darkness (209e2–5). And blind does he appear, for he quickly realizes that, for an opinion to be true on this account, it must already contain knowledge of the difference of one thing from all else, otherwise one could hardly distinguish Socrates from Theaetetus (209e6–210a6). Like the second definition of an account, the third returns us to the first, in which the account only gives us a reflection of what we already opined. Socrates is thus

---

[25] For my more thorough discussion of this passage, see Priou 2018a, 182–89.

[26] That Socrates anticipates the dialogue will end in failure is clear from a number of moments: he is on the last of his three proposals for what a λόγος would have to be to turn a true opinion into knowledge (208b11–c6), he then mentions mid-argument that they may meet up the next day (209c9), he next concludes the argument as though it wraps up both this definition and the prior two (210a7–b2), and the whole time he knows that he must soon leave in order to receive Meletus' indictment (210d2–4).

brought back to the privacy of perception, extended now beyond perception to all appearance and opining, in an unanticipated and decisive return to Protagorean relativism. Protagoras has nudged, prodded, and now shaken the dozing Socrates awake. Socrates does not fly high above the city in a freedom borne of his leisure, but dwells with Protagoras in the Hades-esque prison of political life (see *Protagoras* 315b9). This is Protagoras' powerful rejoinder to Socrates' hubristic celebration; but it is also a tragic depiction of man's place in the cosmos. With this dark triumph of conventionalism, Act Two draws to a close.

IV.

Our tragic reading of the *Theaetetus* features a Socrates at once impressive and arrogant. Searching among the isolationist mathematicians—those who keep to themselves and their chosen studies—for a mathematical talent still not yet rid of his youthful pliability, Socrates encounters his primary interlocutor, Theaetetus, whom he tries to win to the philosopher's way of life, a soaring freedom spent among the grandeur of the cosmos and away from the pettiness of political concerns. In his exorcism of Protagoras' ghost from Theaetetus' still salvageable soul, Socrates evokes our admiration. For, purged of Protagoras, Theaetetus would be and (Socrates estimates) now *is* prepared to offer up something new as a definition of knowledge in the future (210b11–c2). It is for this reason, we presume, that Socrates suggests they reconvene at dawn for further conversation (210d3). As for the present conversation, however, Socrates' exorcism has proven ineffective, as his lapses in the argument expose his failure to meet his own standard of philosophic rigor and thoroughness. Socrates' attempt to define what knowledge is, beyond perception, has floundered and thus hollowed out his critique of Protagoras' claim to expertise. Protagoras gets his revenge, with all of Socrates' behavior—his threats to expose his interlocutors as asses, his prodding of the reluctant Theaetetus to answer, and his wicked badgering of Theodorus to enter the conversation—serving as evidence in favor of Protagoras' judgment that Socrates is unjust in speech, that he is but another sophist. So, however impressive and admirable we may find Socrates' discoveries, we cannot help but interpret the discrepancy between his vision of philosophy and his actual behavior as a mark of his high-minded hubris. The man who celebrated his freedom from the city now finds himself trapped within its cave no less than anyone else but all the worse prepared to answer the coming charges of impiety and corrupting the youth. Socrates has failed to follow Parmenides' advice to train thoroughly, so as to be prepared to respond to the skeptic; he has ignored the warning of Aristophanes that, in busying himself with cosmic questions, Socrates will discover all too well and much too late the wrath of the city; and he has underestimated Protagoras' claim that he and Socrates differ only in degree, and even then still to Socrates' disadvantage. Not one of these signs slows Socrates. This reading of the *Theaetetus*—again, admittedly flat in its seriousness and inattention to irony—is what gives Theodorus, when he greets Socrates in the *Sophist*, the temerity to instruct the newly indicted Athenian about what makes for a philosopher and how philosophers avoid Socrates' strife-ridden speeches (τὰς ἔριδας) (*Sophist* 216a1–c1). With his tragic fall complete, Socrates encounters the Stranger from Elea, a near *deus ex machina* for Theodorus. In his patricide of father Parmenides, the Stranger will prove relentless where Socrates was hesitant; and in his logical solution to the problem of false opinion, he will emerge victorious where Socrates encountered defeat.

II

SOPHIST

I.

The *Theaetetus* was, by Socrates' own admission, a failure, or at the very least incomplete; and it was for this reason, perhaps, that Socrates arranged with Theodorus for them to meet again on the following morning at dawn (*Theaetetus* 210d3). When Theodorus shows up, however, he is not alone, but brings with him an anonymous Stranger from Elea, whom Theodorus pointedly, even proudly calls "a man very much a philosopher" (μάλα...ἄνδρα φιλόσοφον) (216a1–4).[1] This opening remark tells Socrates all he needs to know. "This man, Socrates, is what we've been looking for," Theodorus implies in his indelicacy. "He, and not you, embodies the philosophic freedom of which you spoke yesterday." Socrates takes the hint, responding that he fears that the Stranger is a refutative god come to punish them for being paltry (φαύλους) in speeches (216a5–b6). As we noted in the Overture, Socrates refers here to that moment in the *Theaetetus* when the bottom appeared to drop out from their conversation as a whole, threatening to expose how paltry (φαῦλοι) they were (*Theaetetus* 196d2–12, esp. d8: πᾶς ἡμῖν ἐξ ἀρχῆς ὁ λόγος; 197a3–4). Socrates remarked then that they have long been filled up with impure conversing (*Theaetetus* 196d12–e2: ἀνάπλεῳ τοῦ μὴ καθαρῶς διαλέγεσθαι). Theodorus thus promises that the Stranger will purify their conversation, freeing it of the sophistry in which Socrates found himself mired—in

---

[1] Unless noted otherwise, all references in this chapter are to the *Sophist*.

which he had mired himself.² Theodorus is quick to correct Socrates' hope that the Stranger is a refutative god by remarking that this "man very much a philosopher" is not a god but divine and, in addition, more measured (μετριώτερος) than those inclined to strife (ἔριδας) (216b7–c1). "You are confused, Socrates, about what philosophy is," Theodorus' indelicacy again says. "Let this man here set you straight."³

In response to Theodorus' implicit promise that the Stranger could correct him about what philosophy is, Socrates reports what his lifetime of experience has led him to conclude about the relationship between the philosopher and the city, according to which experience the philosopher cannot help but appear now and again under the dueling and distortive apparitions (φαντάσματα) of sophist and statesman, as they ineluctably arise on account of the ignorance of the city's denizens (216c2–d2).⁴ Socrates has been used

---

² "In the *Cratylus*, Socrates predicts that on the following day (the day on which the *Sophist* will take place) he and his companions will discover a 'priest or sophist' who is 'clever in purifying' his 'daimonic wisdom'" (Howland 1998, 4). On philosophizing φαύλως in the *Theaetetus*, see Howland 1998, 60.

³ "It is as if [Theodorus] does not want to risk being pressured yet again by Socrates to engage in philosophic discussion. Instead, he brings with him a new addition to the company, the Eleatic Stranger, who will soon take over the discussion. Theodorus brings in a 'hired gun,' as it were, to take care of this Socrates and his irritating habit of questioning!" (Hyland 2017, 228; see 228–29 as a whole). The Stranger seems to follow Theodorus' expectations here: "The Eleatic does not ask his interlocutor to state his own opinion and then examine it the way Socrates does. The Eleatic proposes a statement or alternatives and asks his interlocutor whether he agrees or disagrees. His method of interrogation is thus much less confrontational than Socrates'. As a result it has a different effect. Culminating in an agreement on the definition of a term, it does not produce the kind of perplexity (*aporia*) that Theaetetus experienced the day before" (Zuckert 2009, 687). See, however, Section II, paragraph four.

⁴ In addition to the philosopher's φαντάσματα of sophist and statesman, Socrates also mentions that he occasionally furnishes the opinion that he is altogether mad (216c8–d2). The only other time that madness is mentioned in the *Sophist* is when the Stranger confesses to Theaetetus that he is afraid he

to laying blame for his occasional ventures into sophistry on the ignorance of others and on the city at large. But by asking in the *Theaetetus* what knowledge is, Socrates appears unwittingly to have discovered, with Theodorus and Theaetetus as witnesses, that his knowledge is no less a shadow than the opinions of the city and therewith exposed himself as no less a cave-dweller than those around him. If the Stranger is to fulfill Theodorus' promise and embody the philosophic freedom Socrates praised but ultimately lacks, then he must, as he will, oppose Socrates' view by maintaining that these three men—philosopher, sophist and statesman—can, with effort and patience, be distinguished from one another as three independent beings to the common lights of the city (217a5–e5). The Stranger's alternative—elaborated, we recall, in accordance with Theodorus' wishes and thus in obedience to Zeus' law of guest-friendship (ξενία)—effectively amounts to a promissory assertion that the ignorance Socrates mentioned can be overcome and that the philosopher can, before all, distinguish himself adequately from the sophist.

A quick glance at what the Stranger accomplishes in the *Sophist* appears to show that he does, indeed, deliver on his promissory assertion. For he succeeds not only in defining the sophist separate from the philosopher, but in the process he also takes on the thought of Parmenides and solves the problem of false opinion, succeeding precisely where Socrates failed in the *Theaetetus*; further, the Stranger's solution appears logical rather than analogical, avoiding thereby the lapse into the impurity of images that Socrates so lamented as a stain on their conversation; likewise, he appears to succeed in offering a Theodoran alternative to Protagoras' and Socrates'

---

will seem to be mad, should he shift his position back-and-forth at every step (παρὰ πόδα μεταβαλὼν ἐμαυτὸν ἄνω καὶ κάτω) (242a10–b2). If thinking is "the conversation without voice that comes to be within the soul with itself" (263e3–5), that is, the personification of two positions in a back-and-forth exchange within a single person, then the external voicing of this conversation risks appearing as a sort of schizophrenia. Certainly, some first-time readers of Plato have this experience.

competing views of expertise, by way of his method of division and its proto-modern treatment of the true in distinction from the good (227a7–b6);[5] and, as if all this weren't enough, the Stranger also articulates a preliminary vision of an alternative to the impurity of Socrates in the form of the one who philosophizes both purely and justly (τῷ καθαρῶς τε καὶ δικαίως φιλοσοφοῦντι), a philosopher in possession of a "dialectical science" (διαλεκτικὴ ἐπιστήμη) (253d1–e6) and who actually attains the purity and freedom Socrates celebrated in speech but failed to live up to in deed (253c7–9: τὴν τῶν ἐλευθέρων...ἐπιστήμην; see *Theaetetus* 175d8–e1, 177a5). Whereas by the end of the *Theaetetus* Protagoras had dragged Socrates down to his level, the Stranger here appears to succeed in redeeming philosophy from the sophist's attack. The Stranger thus exposes Socrates' worst nightmare as all-too-real, that his life-long recourse to the occasional sophistic trick was needless and that he consequently merits the very punishment he now knows he risks receiving (see *Euthyphro* 2d4–3a2).

Such is what we expect, at least, when we take our bearings by Theodorus' anticipation. But regardless of whether the dialogue delivers on this anticipation, it is no doubt clear that, confused or not,

---

[5] "Socrates has sought to divide things hierarchically into better and worse kinds (according to their closeness or distance from the good) rather than sorting them horizontally, the way the Eleatic himself does, into same and other" (Zuckert 2009, 681; see 702 for the connection with non-being as the other, as well as 705). As Howland notes, the Stranger's "explicit pronouncements concerning the method of bifurcatory division regularly conflict with his actual employment of this method" (Howland 1998, 6). Thus, Blitz hesitates to assert either a complete difference between or the complete identity of the two men (Blitz 2010, 263–67). On the connection between the Stranger's method of division and arithmetic, see Howland 1998, 185–86. See, also, Hyland 2017, 227.—The method here is deductive not inductive, though they finally emphasize the priority of induction in the *Statesman* during the third methodological digression, in which the Stranger concedes that any demonstration (ἀπόδειξις) necessarily invokes examples or models (παραδείγματα)—that is, all general distinctions are based, inductively, on "data."

Socrates is certainly confusing. His sophistry is not so simple as, say, Protagoras' explicit and avowed brand (*Protagoras* 316d3–317c5; see 311a5–7). Indeed, as Theodorus now reveals and Socrates likely perceived, he and the Stranger had already been discussing on their way over the very topic that Socrates just introduced of his own accord (216d3–217b2). One suspects that it was Theodorus' seminal experience of Socrates the day before that generated this prior discussion, for in taking the Stranger to Socrates Theodorus surely had to explain who Socrates is and what happened yesterday that necessitated a second meeting today.[6] And when we reflect back on that conversation in light of their discussion of the philosopher's similarity to and difference from the sophist and statesman, we cannot help but see in Socrates' behavior glimpses of both apparitions. Socrates was no doubt sophistic in his badgering Theodorus to join the conversation and his maligning too hastily Protagoras' orphaned speech, to name but two of the many transgressions we encountered. But Socrates was not simply sophistic: it was he himself who took himself to task for his treatment of Protagoras, as Theodorus too recognized; likewise, Theaetetus was quite impressed with all that Socrates had helped him accomplish by the end of the dialogue, despite not attaining their goal of defining what knowledge is (*Theaetetus* 168c2–7, 210b6–7). In these respects, Socrates seems to be one of those who resemble the statesman in nurturing others (see *Statesman* 268a6–d1). The failures of the *Theaetetus* thus prove to prompt the question of the relationship between the sophist, the statesman, and the philosopher, the very question the *Sophist* and *Statesman* are to answer. Consequently, these twin dialogues aren't simply a correction of Socrates' confusion. Rather, they are at the same time and more fundamentally an exploration of Socrates himself, of his way of life as a phenomenon, of his confounding appearance. Together they convey the problem of Socrates.[7]

---

[6] As notes Benardete 2000, 299–300.
[7] For my earlier articulation of this feature, see Priou 2018a, 204–6.

Understood thus, Socrates' desire to learn from the Stranger can also be seen as his challenge to this Eleatic interloper to escape the problem in which Socrates has found himself. The Stranger's reluctance at the magnitude of his task is therefore warranted (217b1–4), for it will be no mean feat if he can deliver on his promissory assertion that the sophist and philosopher can indeed be separated from one another. Will the Stranger successfully escape the problem of Socrates? As we have seen, there is good reason to expect he will, but still, we should not be too hasty, for it is this *attempt* at escape that drives the drama of the *Sophist* and that we will retell in the present chapter. The Stranger will first encounter this problem in the sophist's slipperiness, as he dons many guises, the most perplexing being that of the purifying, refutative sophist, who seems like a perfected form of Socrates from the *Theaetetus*; to sort the two out, the Stranger will distinguish "spoken images" (εἴδωλα λεγόμενα) into those that distort the beings (φαντάσματα) and those that preserve their proportions (εἰκόνες), in order eventually to distinguish true opinions from false and so the philosopher from his spurious counterpart in the sophist (Section II).[8] As the Stranger makes his way in his attempted escape, he will confront his philosophic father Parmenides, the omission of whose thought proved so ruinous to Socrates' argument in the *Theaetetus*; but lest we take this confrontation and its apparent successes as a sign that the Stranger has escaped the problem of Socrates, the Stranger suddenly though quietly stumbles upon the difficulty, if not impossibility, of acquiring the pure and just philosopher's dialectical science, without which such escape is impossible (Section III). The stumble will prove no

---

[8] There are no clear English equivalents to these terms, so I have resorted to using the phrases "distortive apparition" for φάντασμα and "accurate semblance" for εἰκών, borrowing and expanding the translation adopted by Benardete 1984. For εἰκαστική and φανταστική, I will use the phrases "art of making semblances" or "accurate semblances" and "art of making apparitions" or "distortive apparitions." On occasion, as just below, I will adjust these phrases for clarity and ease of discussion, always including, however, the Greek terms parenthetically as reminders to the reader in these cases.

Sophist

less ruinous for the Stranger than for Socrates, as the dialogue's three positive conclusions—the identification of non-being with the other, the account of false opinion, and the final definition of the sophist—will prove to be apparitions (φαντάσματα), that is, latently analogical, and thus no escape from the sophist's distortive spoken images (Section IV). To escape the problem of Socrates through the apparition (φάντασμα) of the sophist will thus prove impossible. Thankfully, the apparition of the statesman will promise another way out.

II.

Whereas Socrates began his conversation with Theaetetus with an ambitious question and an aggressive, if playful, demeanor, the Stranger proposes to start with something small and work his way up to what is great: his approach is more gradual and accommodating. What they soon discover, however, is that the sophist's complexity is such as to throw Theaetetus into perplexity (ἀπορία).[9] It is this perplexity that initiates the dialogue's digression and so elucidates the motivation underlying their inquiry. Our first task, therefore, must be to understand the nature of the perplexity that the Stranger induces in the young Theaetetus, if thereafter we are to understand adequately both the distinction of spoken images into distortive apparitions (φαντάσματα) and accurate semblances (εἰκόνες) and the consequent need to acquire the dialectical science. That is, because the digression departs from and returns to this perplexity, these initial attempts at defining the sophist cast their shadow over the conversation as a whole. Not until the concluding

---

[9] I have reluctantly translated ἀπορία both here and in subsequent chapters, as it seems to waver between being without provision and being without a way, depending on context. In general, its meaning is closer to "perplexity" in the *Sophist*, while in the *Statesman* it is closer to "being without resource or recourse" (see Chapter III, Section II).

Section IV, then, will we have gained the proper perspective from which to understand this perplexity's import.

The Stranger begins by meeting Theaetetus on his own terms, seducing rather than thrusting him into unknown territory. Toward that end, he approaches their task using something smaller and easier to understand as a model (παράδειγμα), namely, the angler, in accordance with whose features they can then attempt to define the sophist (218c5–219a3).[10] Of course, the attempt to move from the easier to the more difficult is bound to have its complications. Nevertheless, the expectation is that the model of the angler will facilitate the conversation greatly. Their execution of this method appears to affirm this expectation, as there is a noteworthy degree of kinship (221d8–9: συγγενῆ) between the angler and the sophist or correspondence of the sophist with this model (221c6–7: κατὰ τοῦτο τὸ παράδειγμα). Of course, the correspondence extends only so far. For the angler and sophist "together make their way" (πορεύεσθον) through the distinction of the arts into the acquisitive as opposed to the productive, then into mastery as opposed to exchange, then into hunting as opposed to competition, and finally into the hunting of animals or of the ensouled kind as opposed to that of the kind without soul (ἄψυχον); thereafter, however, they part ways, with the sophist hunting on foot and the angler in water (221c6–222a11). The model isn't strict, therefore, but neither need it be for it to be useful, as the discrepancies between the angler and sophist can be no less instructive than their similarities. But a moment of poetic flourish in the Stranger's procedure reveals a deeper difficulty. The Stranger refers to the sophist as hunting "on earth and in turn in certain (τινας) other rivers, bounteous meadows, as it were (οἷον), of wealth and youth" (222a9–10). If the Stranger were to focus on wealth rather than youth here, he would deny that the sophist hunts something ensouled but rather claim that he hunts

---

[10] For a synoptic account of the role of παραδείγματα in Plato, see Patterson 1985, 11–23. For some patterns in the Stranger's use of them, see the helpful account in Gill 2012, 141–42.

something without soul, thus decreasing the correspondence. But if he adopted the metaphor of rivers rather than meadows, he would increase the correspondence, since both angler and sophist would hunt in a sort of water. Thus, in the apparently quite simple description of and extrapolation from a model, the Stranger stumbles across the basic issue of the dialogue's digression, namely, the complex manner in which images obscure the kinds (γένη), even as they illuminate them.[11]

The Stranger remains gentle with Theaetetus, introducing him to the sophist's trickery by having him don a number of guises. The angler model gives them the first sophist, the hunter of wealth and youth. The Stranger is unsatisfied, however, as the preceding makes the sophist's art seem slight or paltry (φαύλης), when in fact it is quite motley or complex (ποικίλης) (223c1–2). It is the sophist's complexity that the Stranger seeks to impress upon Theaetetus as an intermediary step on the way to the more daunting question of the ground of this complexity in the problem of images. The Stranger shows Theaetetus a series of the sophist's guises. After the hunter sophist, we encounter the merchant of speeches and lessons on virtue (224c9–d3). They then immediately stumble on the third, the retailer of another's lessons or seller of his own (καπηλικὸν εἴτε αὐτοπωλικόν) (224d4–e5). Fourth is the competitive sophist, someone who engages in linguistic combat for pay (226a1–5). Theaetetus is struck by the sophist's new, eristic appearance, calling him a marvel or wonder (θαυμαστὸν) (225e3–5). Theodorus, we surmise, sees Socrates here (compare 216b8). The Stranger can thus confirm with Theaetetus that he has come to appreciate his earlier claim, that "it's truly said that this beast is complex" (ποικίλον) and that the sophist is not to be seized casually (226a6–8). The Stranger

---

[11] Hence Speliotis rightly questions (and sees Theaetetus as skeptical about) whether the sophist is a hunter: "Far from being a neutral, 'objective' observation of what is manifest and apparent, by characterizing the sophist as a hunter of human beings, the Stranger seems to be importing and imposing certain judgments and presuppositions on the phenomena" (Speliotis 2013, 202).

thus uses the rapid proliferation of the sophist's guises to bring Theaetetus to see his complexity but—crucially—while keeping the core perplexity at bay. That is, the Stranger induces in Theaetetus an experience of the challenge images pose to thinking but at a distance from its root cause in the difficulty of assessing their distortion of being and their consequently peculiar status with respect to being and non-being. Whereas Socrates had scared Theaetetus into silence, the Stranger has maintained Theaetetus' interest in the search by only gradually introducing him to the problems ahead.

According to Theaetetus' experience so far, the problem of the sophist lies in his capacity to range in appearance from a domesticated, apparently harmless peddler of books to the more troubling predator and pugilist. After the next definition, however, Theaetetus does more than merely confirm for the Stranger the sophist's complexity but expresses of his own accord his perplexity (ἀπορία) in the face of the sophist's ability to deceive them (231b9–c2). It is this definition, then, that will elucidate the concern motivating the dialogue's digression. According to this definition, the sophist purifies the soul of ignorance (ἄγνοια) through refutation, without which purification we would all remain uneducated and ugly—even the Great King of Persia (230d7–e4). The Stranger expresses his reservations along the way (230e6–231a3) but ultimately agrees with some reluctance to call such purification "the well-bred breed of sophistics" (231b8: ἡ γένει γενναία σοφιστική).[12] The cause of perplexity thus appears to be that the sophist now ranges not just from predator to peddler, as before, but all the way up to godsend (see *Protagoras* 320c2–328d2, esp. 322c1–3 with 328a8–b5). That is, in addition to simply multiplying himself, the sophist is also able to

---

[12] Theaetetus, for his part, is not as reluctant as the Stranger to call this noble purifier a sophist. He has, after all, spent quite some time undergoing this purgation himself, as Socrates yesterday disabused him of a number of inadequate definitions of knowledge. But he has also spent quite some time hearing Theodorus speak disapprovingly of Socrates' behavior, both to Socrates' face and behind his back. Socrates is not so noble as this sophist.

don guises both noble and base—to seem like a sort of super-Socrates performing the greatest of benefactions even to the most exalted in the city (see *Apology of Socrates* 30a5–7). Though Socrates had indeed only a little earlier presented himself as different from the city's denizens in terms of their ignorance (ἄγνοια), he had done so while expressing his own need for refutation (see 216a5–b6, c2–d2). And though Socrates had, the day before, characterized the philosopher as occupying a pure place, still he admitted thereafter to a fear that he has been conversing impurely—and, in reality, not just now but his whole life (*Theaetetus* 177a5, 196d11–e9). Theaetetus is thus made to concern himself with rescuing from the sophist a purer form of Socratic philosophy, one Socrates preached but admittedly did not practice—with making a newer, nobler Socrates.

The close juxtaposition of the combative, eristic sophist to the purifying, refuter sophist certainly echoes the tension between Socrates' twin apparitions (φαντάσματα). But Theaetetus' perplexity is more morally motivated. With Theaetetus perplexed, the Stranger in his agreeableness offers that they take a breather and survey the terrain traversed by enumerating the various apparitions (φαντάσματα) of the sophist they've glimpsed. The enumerations have puzzled readers, as the present tally differs from the one they kept during the earlier discussion.[13] Theaetetus initially had the count at four (225e3–5), which implies that the noble sophist brings the total to five. But after the sophist's latest appearance as a noble purifier of ignorance, Theaetetus interrupts the Stranger mid-enumeration so as to add a new fourth, "the seller of his own lessons" (231d10–11: αὐτοπώλης περὶ τὰ μαθήματα), thus bringing the total to six. The Stranger had mentioned the "seller of his own" (αὐτοπώλης) but lumped him together with the retailer as the third (224d4–e4). Thus, in light of Theaetetus' perplexity upon hearing of the noble sophist and his subsequent emphasis of the "seller of his own," one is tempted to understand Theaetetus' perplexity as

---

[13] For a discussion, see Howland 1998, 193–96.

morally motivated. More precisely, the Stranger's neologism of αὐτοπώλης might sound to Theaetetus less as "seller of one's own things" than as "seller of himself," that is, as signifying one who, like a prostitute, commodifies himself, namely, through a commodification of what he has learned for himself. Indeed, the pejorative word for a prostitute, πόρνη, derives from πέρνημι, "to sell." Further, the Greeks tended to distinguish ἑταῖραι, "courtesans," from πόρναι, "prostitutes," along the lines of the Stranger's distinction between exchange for gifts and exchange for money, by which distinction he arrived at the merchant sophist (223c9–d5).[14] Theaetetus—an eager learner who is notably liberal with money and inexperienced in erotic matters (222d10–11, *Theaetetus* 143d1–144d7)—would certainly find the sophist's prostituting of his own lessons (μαθήματα) to anyone willing to pay the price worthy of reproach and so would also find the appearance of the streetwalker as the city's savior a cause of great perplexity. Theaetetus' problem concerns not so much how the pugilist lays claim to purification as how someone could dare to prostitute purification—to sell indulgences, as it were.

The Stranger next elaborates on the perplexity in which Theaetetus finds himself. Given the number and range of apparitions (φαντάσματα) that the sophist has assumed, he and Theaetetus reasonably conclude that they have proven "incapable of looking upon" (οὐ δύναται κατιδεῖν) his art (232a1–7). Their incapacity is the result of the sophist's own capacity, namely, "an adequate capacity (δύναμις) with respect to disputation about all things" (232e2–4). They rightly agree that the sophist would have to be a god to deliver on his promise of omniscience (232e6–233a4; see 233c1–9, 234b5–6). Their doubt thus leads them to pose the question of how these men, though lacking such knowledge, are nevertheless "capa-

---

[14] There is a vast body of literature on what distinguished the pejorative πόρνη from the more courteous and dignified ἑταίρα in the Greeks' minds, and whether their respective statuses were considerably different in reality. I have found most helpful Kurke 1997.

ble (δυνατοὶ) of furnishing the young with the opinion or reputation (δόξαν) that they," that is, the sophists, "are wisest of all in all things" (233b1–2). The Stranger refers to this deed as "the wonder of the sophistic capacity" (233a8–9: τὸ τῆς σοφιστικῆς δυνάμεως θαῦμα). From such a capacity the sophist is capable of misleading the thoughtless among the young into thinking that he is most competent in whatever he wishes to do (234b5–10). The sophist is thus primarily a sort of sorcerer or charlatan, who bewitches or beguiles the young with his "spoken images" (234c2–5, 234e7–235a7).[15] That is, Theaetetus is brought to wonder how the sophist's spoken images allow him to appear, not just as the noble sophist with an art of purging souls of ugliness, but as god himself. This illusory nobility or beauty is an example of "what appears to resemble the beautiful (τὸ φαινόμενον...ἐοικέναι τῷ καλῷ) because the viewing [is] not from [a] beautiful [position or person] (οὐκ ἐκ καλοῦ)" (236b4–5). That is, it is the very ugliness of the soul called ignorance (228e1–5: ἄγνοια) that allows the sophist to convince the young like Theaetetus (see 234c2–e4, 239e1) that his art is "the greatest and most authoritative purification" in the city (230d7–9), that allows the self-seller (αὐτοπώλης) to appear as a refutative god. Thus, when the Stranger introduces this distinction in kinds of images, it will be from Theaetetus' perspective, that of a youth captivated by the sophist's advertisement of an ennobling education in virtue but with misgivings about the moral rectitude of his enterprise (see *Protagoras* 310b4–8, 311d4–312a7).[16]

---

[15] The Stranger uses the ambiguous γόης, which implies both magic and trickery, as the above dualities of sorcerer/charlatan and bewitch/beguile are meant to reflect. The ambiguity neatly parallels the experience of the thoughtless young and the mindfully doubtful. For an example of the philosopher appearing as γόης, see *Meno* 79e7–80b7 and context.

[16] Contrary to what commentators often suppose, then, it is not solely the multiplicity of definitions that motivates the Stranger and Theaetetus on the dialogue's digression but the moral difference between them. The reason for this oversight seems to be the Stranger's emphasis on multiplicity at

Accordingly, in order to resolve the perplexity induced by the sophist's range of appearances from base to noble, the Stranger must make his distinction of "spoken images" into distortive apparitions (φαντάσματα) and accurate semblances (εἰκόνες). In so doing, he necessarily treads upon the problem of Socrates, of his peculiar but as yet incomprehensible mixture of these two forms.[17] Should the Stranger and Theaetetus succeed in saving the purifying sophist from his prostituting pretender, will Socrates, we wonder, be saved along with him or cast aside with the chaff?[18] Only if the Stranger can actually make this distinction will he be able to distinguish true opinions from false and so succeed where Socrates failed; one wonders, too, whether his method of division could still remain indifferent to the good as it ascends to the true. Be that as it may, as the Stranger turns now to his task, he expresses some trepidation about his ability to accomplish it, saying, "I, for one, appear to myself (ἔγωγέ μοι...φαίνομαι) even now to look upon (καθορᾶν) two forms (εἴδη) of mimetics. But the look (ἰδέαν) being sought, in which of our two [forms] it ever happens to be, I seem to myself (μοι δοκῶ) not yet to be capable (δυνατὸς) of understanding (καταμαθεῖν)" (235d1–3). The Stranger's highly subjective language, in addition to his general hesitation, is not reassuring. And though the phrase "not yet" may give us some additional hope in the ensuing discussion, the Stranger will not have reached clarity on this

---

232a1–7 (see, for example, Gill 2012, 145–49). Nevertheless, we must understand such methodological remarks in the context of the Stranger's agreement to obey Zeus' law of ξενία by expanding upon Theodorus' critique of Socrates.

[17] For a helpful discussion of where Socrates has lurked in the various divisions, see Howland 1998, 188–97.

[18] It is noteworthy that Socrates had suggested just the day before that his "midwifery," in pairing youths with more suitable teachers than himself, could be mistaken for pimping (*Theaetetus* 150a1–5). Might he not have also been aware that, in coupling with those youths himself, he'd appear to be, if not a prostitute, at the very least a bit too promiscuous? Compare Strauss 2001, 135 with Bloom 2001, 108; see, also, Benardete 2000, 198.

point by the end of his articulation of the distinction, where he recalls this moment and reaffirms his confusion at the sophist's wondrous capacity to evade capture (236c9–d4). We must temper any hope we may have had that his articulation of this distinction might have offered us a clear path toward separating the sophist from the philosopher.[19] This passage is not so much a solution to as it is a restatement of the problem.

Theaetetus takes this perplexity to heart, noting that he is among those whose age leaves them susceptible to deception (234e3–4). Assuring Theaetetus that all his elders present will aid him by "leading him forward as near as possible without the experiences" of the sophist, the Stranger begins elaborating the distinction of spoken images into apparitions (φαντάσματα) and semblances (εἰκόνες) (234e5–7). Turning first to the art of making semblances (εἰκαστική), the Stranger notes that the generation of such an imitation occurs "whenever [the image is] in accordance with the proportions of the model" (κατὰ τὰς τοῦ παραδείγματος συμμετρίας) (235d6–e2). The difficulties with and eventual breakdown of the image of the sophist constructed on the model of the angler suffice to induce admiration for such an image-maker, if not outright skepticism at the possibility of his task of generating direct correspondence between image and model. Setting the semblance-making art (εἰκαστική) aside, the Stranger then remarks that for fashioning great works the craftsmen let the truth go and so produce not the proportions that *are* but those that seem to be beautiful (235e5–236a6). This species of mimetics (μιμητική) is called the art of producing apparitions (φανταστική). Such image-making (εἰδωλοποιική), sophistry included, compensates, as noted earlier, for the fact that "the viewing [of the image is] not from [a] beautiful

---

[19] The philosopher is not mentioned in the discussion of images. Indeed, he is hardly mentioned outside of the prologue and discussion of the dialectical science (see 216a4, 216c1, 216c6, 217a4, 249c10, 253c9, 253e5, 253e7, 254a8, 259e2, 260a6–7). But the capacity of the pure and just philosopher's dialectical science to see great things adequately, and thus to distinguish φαντάσματα from εἰκόνες, permits this association.

[position or person]" (236b4–5). Thus, for example, the proportions of the statue of Abraham Lincoln at the Lincoln Memorial are distorted so as to accommodate for the distorting place from which a citizen views him. If the actual proportions of the statue were observed, the head would appear far greater than that of Lincoln himself, like a sort of presidential homunculus. Thus, as a corrective to the sophistic capacity, one would need, as the Stranger puts it, to "seize a capacity to see adequately things of such a size" (236b5–6: δύναμιν ἱκανῶς ὁρᾶν). Among things of such a size one includes not just the "great works" (μέγαλα ἔργα) but also—and in the case of the sophist, especially and specifically—the "greatest kinds" (μέγιστα γένη), that is, those beings with which the dialectical science concerns itself (254c1–4, d4–6).

So explained, the distinction is readily understood. But when the Stranger remarks on the process by which these images are produced, a difficulty arises. Now, Theaetetus and the Stranger are attempting to discover and elude the sophistic capacity of deception, toward which end they must acquire a capacity to see great things adequately. The latter capacity cannot be acquired, however, unless we understand how the model or original is distorted in the process of becoming an apparition (φάντασμα). Unfortunately, this process is not altogether apparent from what the Stranger gives us. Rather, all he says is that, should the maker of an apparition "give off the true proportions of the beautiful things," they will appear distorted or deformed—that is, ugly (235e6–7; see 228a10–11). Though brief, this statement is nevertheless revealing. We initially presume that the apparition-maker constructs an apparition by adjusting the proportions of the model *as it is* so that they are more beautiful to the viewer. Instead, however, he says the proportions are not of the beings but of the beautiful things.[20] That is, the Stranger suggests

---

[20] Badham's proposed emendation of τὴν τῶν καλῶν ἀληθινὴν συμμετρίαν to read τὴν τῶν κώλων ἀληθινὴν συμμετρίαν "avoids language that would blur the point required," as notes Robinson 1999, 145. But just

that our grasp of the model is already mediated by images, that "the true proportions" may not be of the beings but only of the beautiful things, that our grasp of the model risks having the proportions of an apparition (φάντασμα). As the Stranger's phrase "that which appears to resemble the beautiful" (τὸ φαινόμενον ἐοικέναι τῷ καλῷ) clearly indicates (236b4–5), what appears to be a semblance of a being (εἰκὼν ὄντος) risks being a semblance of an apparition (εἰκὼν φαντάσματος). For, so long as what is must always appear to be—and we can only know that something is if it appears to be—the sophist has his room to play. But if that's so, how will the Stranger ever separate the sophist from the philosopher? And so, by extension, how could Socrates ever be culpable for someone with poor vision mistaking him for a sophist?[21]

What the Stranger's language suggests (but so far *only* suggests) is that the necessary supervenience of appearance on being means there is a horizon to discerning whether an image is a distortive apparition (φάντασμα) or an accurate semblance (εἰκών). This suggestion promises to redeem the problem of Socrates, inasmuch as it collapses sophistry with philosophy, but at the price of understanding philosophy as necessarily impure. That is, it is questionable whether one should prioritize semblances over apparitions, as the Stranger does, since the former evinces knowledge of being while the latter evinces additionally knowledge of soul. Likewise, it is questionable whether there is, as the Stranger appears to assume, a simply beautiful position from which no distortion occurs (236b4–5; compare *Symposium* 210e2–211b5 against 212a2–5). Comprehensive knowledge of the whole would seem to require combining both arts of image-making, impossible as it may seem. Socratic refutation, in its elicitation of the incoherence in our opinions and their

---

such a blur pervades the dialogue as its principal difficulty, namely, the obstacle the beautiful poses to adequate sight of reality. The fact that the true proportions inhere in something beautiful is an important, early anticipation of the problems articulated later in the text and elaborated in Sections III and IV. On the mathematical language here, see Howland 1998, 210–11.

[21] On Socratic punishment and culpable ignorance, see Berman 2018.

failure to capture the complexity of reality, seems to point to soul and world at once and so achieve the desired combination. Not until the end of Chapter Four will be in a position to understand this combination. For now, the Stranger is engaged in an attempt, however futile, to rescue semblances from the impurity of apparitions and for this reason bookends his discussion by remarking that he lacks the capacity to discern which art to assign to the sophist, the semblance-making or the apparition-making art (235c9–d3, 236c9–10). This remark is intelligible only if the distinction between apparition and semblance is somehow uncertain, that is, only if the Stranger worries that there is no accessible basis on which to draw this distinction.[22] The sophist's claim to make true images may be suspicious, but it is not as yet demonstrably false. In this spirit, the Stranger remarks at the very end of the passage that the sophist has fled into an impassable species (ἄπορον εἶδος), a look or form that offers no recourse for escaping its ambiguity (236d1–3). Nevertheless, the conversation proceeds on the presupposition that the two arts can indeed be separated, so that the species (εἶδος) is not without its way through (πόρος). Such a way is available only if we can acquire a capacity to see great things adequately. This capacity is

---

[22] Following Aristotle's model in *Nicomachean Ethics* VI.1, one could well argue that the distinction between the two εἴδη of images can be made, but the identification of a particular image as a member of one εἶδος or the other is impossible. But adequate sight of the εἴδη is precisely what is in question here. To use Howland's formulation, the Stranger's "uncertainty seems to be connected with the difficulties that arise when the percipient soul is taken into account" (Howland 1998, 209). The sophist denies that anything is one in itself (see *Protagoras* 334a3–c6, *Theaetetus* 152d2–3), a challenge the philosopher must face if his activity is to be possible (see *Parmenides* 134e9–135c6). Thus, Aristotle only claims that there is a science of being after having confronted the "most difficult and necessary ἀπορία of all to look into," namely, whether or not "there is something (ἔστι τι) aside from the particulars," "something one and the same (ἕν τι καὶ ταὐτόν)" that would make such a science possible (see Aristotle, *Metaphysics* B.4.999a24–29, Γ.1.1003a21–22). The sophist poses a radical challenge to the philosopher precisely by denying the possibility of distinguishing their speeches.

what the Stranger will call the dialectical science. Can the attempt to acquire the dialectical science overcome the horizon suggested above? Only if it can will philosophy be purged of sophistry, the Stranger be shown victorious over Socrates, and the *Theaetetus* remain for us a tragedy. Otherwise, the Stranger's Theodoran critique of Socrates will have demanded unreasonably, even irrationally, that philosophy be purer than it can be.

Thus, it is not without justification that the Stranger has been so gentle with Theaetetus, as *we* well know from Theaetetus' silence at Socrates' less accommodating treatment. For the Stranger, however, it is the difficulty of the subject matter itself that risks alienating his young interlocutor. He has done his best to delay Theaetetus' confrontation with it—by practicing with him using something small as a model, by showing him the sophist's complexity before throwing him into perplexity, by offering him some rest from the conversation after he eventually finds himself perplexed, and finally by suppressing the question of whether there is a horizon to our ability to distinguish apparitions from semblances. Now, however, there can be no further delay, for by attempting with Theaetetus to distinguish them finally, the Stranger necessarily treads into forbidding territory. And though the Stranger will continue his procedure of incrementally introducing him to the difficulties, Theaetetus will eventually express his desire to take leave of the conversation should the sophist's trickery not soon end. It is in Theaetetus' resignation, in his unwillingness to work his way through the problem of Socrates, that Socrates will find his redemption from the present accusation of needless sophistry, to say nothing of future ones.

III.

As the Stranger leads Theaetetus deeper into the thicket of perplexities, he remains careful not to overwhelm the youth, who has expressed concern that his age will prevent him from catching the sophist (234e3–4). Emphasizing the difficulty of traversing the perplexity, the Stranger still begins small and works his way up (235c9–

237b6). He first points out that, if to opine falsely is to speak what is not; and if, in addition, whenever we speak we say something (τι) and not nothing (μηδέν); then the person who speaks falsely doesn't even speak (237b7–e6). Theaetetus' reaction is to comment that the argument (λόγος) has reached the perfect or complete end of the perplexity (τέλος...ἀπορίας) (237e7). The Stranger warns him of speaking with confidence too soon (μήπω μέγ' εἴπῃς), promising next the greatest and first of the perplexities (238a1–3). If number is, the Stranger elaborates, then to speak non-being (τὸ μὴ ὄν) alone by itself, as though it were some one thing, is impossible, so that non-being is unthinkable, unsayable, unutterable, and irrational (ἄλογον) (238a4–c11). Theaetetus is impressed but again too soon, as the Stranger feigns surprise at yet another, still greater perplexity beyond this (238c12–d4). For, as the Stranger observes, he himself, in giving these arguments, has been doing what those same arguments forbid him (238d5–239a12). With the perplexities having grown so large—beyond what Theaetetus had expected and the Stranger had feigned to expect himself—the Stranger demurs before the task and asks Theaetetus to assume the helm instead (239b1–5). Shocked at this suggestion, Theaetetus remarks that his eagerness would be out of place (ἄτοπος), even were he to *attempt* to solve what so confounded the Stranger himself as to stop him (239b7–c3). Theaetetus exhibits none of the eagerness that was on display when he ventured into the unforged mathematical terrain that arrested his teacher Theodorus. The superlative courage and eagerness Theodorus praised was, we recall and now reaffirm, peculiarly circumscribed (see Chapter I, Section I). Theaetetus' deference is all the more troubling, for as the Stranger is about to explain to him, they will not be able to catch the sophist, and so find the philosopher, unless they have the daring to kill off his own intellectual father, Parmenides. Such formal deference to one's teacher is an obstacle to philosophy, which requires in certain cases what we will call a *didactic parricide*, the instructive challenging of one's intellectual parentage (see Aristotle, *Nicomachean Ethics* I.6.1096a11–17).[23] The Stranger laments that, with Theaetetus discouraged still more than he, the sophist has sunk down into an impassable place (εἰς ἄπορον...τόπον) (239c4–8). So long as Theaetetus stays in place, the sophist will have his escape.

Theaetetus fully affirms that they will never catch the sophist, so the Stranger next expands upon how the sophist pulled this off. The sophist, here imitated by the Stranger, asks Theaetetus and the Stranger what they mean by the word "image" (εἴδωλον) (238c9–d6). Answering on behalf of himself and the Stranger, Theaetetus is here more confident, offering some examples: reflections in water and mirrors, paintings and sculptures, and the like (239d7–9; see *Theaetetus* 206d1–5). The Stranger is quick to point out Theaetetus' lack of experience with actual sophists, who will claim they are unfamiliar with such things, as though they were in fact blind, requesting instead, on the basis of argument or speech alone, what makes all such experiences one thing (239e1–240a6). Theaetetus responds by defining an image as "something of another sort (τὸ...ἕτερον τοιοῦτον) made similar (ἀφωμοιωμένον) to the true" (240a7–8). Here, the Stranger shows how the sophist evades capture by employing such Parmenidean arguments as he had just summarized for Theaetetus, effectively substituting non-being for otherness (240a9–c1). This substitution is all the more striking, as the Stranger's solution to the problems here raised will be to substitute otherness for non-being. That is, he appears to deliberately complicate the conversation, extending it over twenty pages, for the purpose, we surmise and will soon see, of encouraging Theaetetus. That aside, by speaking here as the sophist, the Stranger attempts to give Theaetetus a mediated experience of the sophist and some confidence in assuming his own role leading their discussion. The Stranger is successful, as Theaetetus readily grasps the difficulty and even begins speaking as the sophist himself, imitating the Stranger's imitation and thus playing all roles (240c2–241b3, esp. 240c2–3,

---

[23] For a helpful discussion of parricide, see Howland 1998, 213.

241a7–b3). Theaetetus is not without his eagerness, then. But it is a qualified eagerness. For as soon as the Stranger notes the extent of the sophist's bag of tricks, that they are nearly limitless (ἀπεράντων), Theaetetus concludes that it's impossible to catch him (241b4–c3).

Despite the impossibility, Theaetetus does agree that they should not go soft, so long as they are able to seize upon him even a little (καὶ κατὰ σμικρὸν) (241c4–6). That is, so long as a path (πόρος) is available, it seems, Theaetetus will take it. Of course, the sophist may prove unable to be seized, if mimetics should turn out to be, as the Stranger worried, an impassable species (ἄπορον εἶδος). If such is the case and the path (πόρος) ends in perplexity (ἀπορία), then Theaetetus will take his leave. As he tells us, he is entirely willing to forgive the Stranger, should he decide to give up (241c7–10). In this way, Theaetetus will prove *ad oculos* Socrates' claim that it is the ignorance of others that necessitates his confusion with the sophist. Or rather, we may now add, it is a necessary ignorance as to whether a speech (λόγος) is a distortive apparition (φάντασμα) or an accurate semblance (εἰκών) that so blurs philosophy and sophistry, an ignorance common, pervasive, and all-too-human. The Stranger's challenge, then, is to keep Theaetetus invested and interested, despite the obstacles they will face both intrinsically given the subject matter and circumstantially on account of Theaetetus' psychological recalcitrance to the proliferation of perplexities. This is no mean challenge, as among the obstacles they face is the apparently impenetrable, seamless logic of Parmenides that the sophist uses to trap his pursuers—the very Parmenides who only moments ago nearly stopped the Stranger and Theaetetus dead in their tracks and before whom just the day before Socrates shrank back from discussing out of reverent awe. As the Stranger warns Theaetetus, he must commit the grave transgression of patricide in daring (τολμητέον) to question father Parmenides' logic (241d1–

242a4).[24] The Stranger thus presents himself as a model for Theaetetus to imitate, that is, as a model of the benefits of didactic parricide. "You may eventually need to do to me," the Stranger suggests to Theaetetus, "what I will soon do to Parmenides." The Stranger's rather clever tactic, then, is to use Theaetetus' deference to undermine itself, for his deference to the Stranger might eventually entail defiance.

The Stranger next delves into the perplexity of being, and his approach is designed to encourage Theaetetus further as they tread into patricidal territory. The Stranger's discussion of those who have offered accounts of being in the past comes in two stages, each with two parts: first he discusses those who say being is two (or some other number) and those who say it is one; then those who say all is body and in becoming, that is, the materialist-fluxists, and those who posit that there are forms, that is, the friends of the forms (τοὺς τῶν εἰδῶν φίλους). With each step, the Stranger offers Theaetetus victory, as flaws in the accounts are readily discerned and those who proffer them thereby surpassed. Those who say being is two—say, hot and cold—are quickly shown to be unable to account for being itself, which appears to be either some third thing, so that being is

---

[24] The Stranger and Theaetetus cannot pursue the sophist unless they have the daring (τόλμα) to go against the "paternal speech" of Parmenides by saying non-being is (237a3–4, 237b7–8, 241a7–b1, 242a1–3). Their daring consists in the attempt to understand the relationship between images and being through a transgression of the law of Parmenides' goddess (see Parmenides B8.32–33). "Daring" has the very same significance in the *Statesman*, where the Stranger argues that the statesman's attempt to change the laws to suit a change in circumstances will be perceived as a daring trespass of the prohibition against acting contrary to the laws or the ancestral and paternal things, themselves an imitation of the statesman's φρόνησις (*Statesman* 295c7–9, 295d2–5, 297d4–e5, 300b1–6; see note 25 to Chapter III). Together, the *Sophist* and *Statesman* suggest that to understand the philosopher requires understanding how the problem the beautiful poses to thinking about being relates to the problem law poses to practical wisdom, by way of the role of images in each problem. Parmenides' goddess seems to be the gatekeeper to this path.

three rather than two, or both together, so that being is one (243d6–244b5). The germ of this logic is then applied to Parmenides, who gives two names—namely, one and being—to what he says is one and, indeed, speaks of the one that is as though it were a whole of parts, so that in both cases it is not one but many (244b6–245d11).[25] Concluding this stage of the discussion, the Stranger notes that those who enumerate the beings—whether as one, two, or however many—will run into unlimited perplexities (ἀπεράντους ἀπορίας) (245d12–e2). Theaetetus responds by asserting rather confidently that any attempt to repair these doctrines will only complicate the problem (245e3–5). The prospect of limitless perplexities, earlier Theaetetus' bogeyman, now inspires his confidence, inasmuch as it is another and not he himself who is so mired.

The Stranger's encouraging tactic continues as they turn to the next pair of doctrines, wherein each argument sees the Stranger and Theaetetus develop their own thesis about being. They first discuss the materialist-fluxists, who hold that all is body and in a state of continual becoming. In their search for a non-bodily counterexample among the things which are, such as justice or virtue, Theaetetus and the Stranger discover that what unites all being, whether bodily or not, is a power or capacity (δύναμις) to affect other things or to be affected by them (246e2–248a3). Likewise, their discussion of the friends of the forms expands upon this hypothesis about being. The friends of the forms hold all to be at rest but must admit to some motion in being, whether it is the motion of cognizing these forms or that of a full-fledged world soul (248a4–249c9; see 265c1–d4). So, the materialist-fluxists unwittingly teach them that being is at rest and bodiless, with the friends of the forms likewise directing

---

[25] Parmenides himself once gave this argument to Socrates, showing that he himself took his own hypothesis that being is one less seriously than the school that arose around him. As the *Parmenides* also shows us, Zeno made this mistake, as well. The Stranger, who appears to be a lapsed Parmenidean (216a2–4; see Cropsey 1995, 69), may have drifted from the dogmas of the school and closer to the thought of the Parmenides himself.

them to see that being is in motion, so that the Stranger and Theaetetus not only dispose of these last two groups but indeed arrive at their very own definition of being as both motion and rest (249c10–d4). Theaetetus affirms this result as most true (249d5: ἀληθέστατα). Thus, at the same time as they have amassed a number of critical victories over all the major schools of the past—not least that of the ever-foreboding Parmenides—they have also recovered from the ashes of these doctrines a novel account of their own. Theaetetus cannot but be encouraged by these results. They certainly exceed what he had accomplished with Socrates the day before.

Of course, we readily discern that the account of being as both motion and rest is subject to the same criticism leveled against those who say being is any pair of contraries, namely, that being appears to be either a third thing in addition to the two or, rather, their unifying principle. This is the very point the Stranger is about to make (see 249e6–250d4). Prior to doing so, however, he pauses to check whether Theaetetus himself has any suspicions, asking, "What, then? Do we already appear (φαινόμεθα) to have suitably (ἐπεικῶς) comprehended being in the argument?" (249d6–7) The Stranger's language here recalls his earlier warning about "what appears to resemble the beautiful" (236b4–5: τὸ φαινόμενον ἐοικέναι τῷ καλῷ). We are reminded, that is, of the horizon to distinguishing a semblance (εἰκών) from an apparition (φάντασμα), a horizon that arises from the necessary supervenience of appearance on being. For, every speech suitable to being at a minimum *appears* to resemble (φαίνεται ἐοικέναι) it and so risks being a mere apparition (φάντασμα). Thus, at the very moment that the Stranger adds another perplexity and so robs Theaetetus of their victory, he points obliquely to the problem of getting an adequate sight on what is always great. Being, the Stranger suggests, is not like a person sighted at a distance, to whom one can get closer, but is seen *only* at a distance and through the same medium: speech (λόγος) with its spoken images (εἴδωλα λεγόμενα). Theaetetus, however, only grows confident when solutions are available. Now robbed of his novel solution to the problem of being, he expresses uncertainty about what direction they can take (250c9–11). For, as things now stand, he considers their perplexity to be the most impossible of all (250d4). Indeed, though the Stranger finds the present perplexity, that of being, equal to that of non-being, Theaetetus despairingly disagrees, holding it to be far greater (250e1–4).[26] In the next stage of the argument, the Stranger and Theaetetus develop the preceding perplexities by considering the application of words to things—more specifically, the degree to which beings partake of one another and thus words can be combined with one another. And throughout, Theaetetus remains unsure of himself—asking for a paradigm, even though this would only repeat the problem of spoken images, and not allowing himself to offer anything on his own unless the question is a rather modest one (251a7, 252d4). The Stranger's predicament is clear: in the absence of an anticipated solution to the perplexities surrounding the sophist, Theaetetus will incline toward accepting defeat. The Stranger can either delve into the problem of Socrates or keep Theaetetus on board, but he cannot do both. It is in this context that the Stranger introduces Theaetetus to the dialectical science.

Continuing the parallel between speech and being, the Stranger proposes the dialectical science as able to accomplish on the level of being what the art of letters (γραμματιστική) accomplishes on the level of language (252e9–253a12). Just as it is necessary to be trained in the art of letters to know which letters can be combined and which cannot, so too "it is necessary for one who is going to make his way (πορεύεσθαι) correctly through the speeches to show with

---

[26] Perhaps, then, what Owen calls "the parity assumption," that is, the "prospect of joint illumination" of the perplexity of being and that of non-being, is not so much "logically…the proper assumption" as it is observationally true (Owen 1999, 421–22). That is, in both speech and deed, the sophist shows us most manifestly how little we understand being. We must understanding being in such a way that it accounts for such perplexities as arise regarding non-being: the problems are one and the same. See the end of Section IV.

some science which of the kinds are consonant with which and which do not accept one another" (253b1–c3). The posited dialectical science promises Theaetetus a way through his impasse. In response, Theaetetus reveals that the source of his earlier hesitance was a longing for a conclusive science of being, saying, "Well, how could there not be a need for a science—and perhaps almost the greatest [science], at that?" (253c4–5) The Stranger discerns the hopefulness in Theaetetus' response, swearing by Zeus at the prospect that they've done the unfathomable, namely, "fallen upon the science of the free" and found the philosopher while still seeking the sophist (253c6–9). It is here that he names this science the dialectical science, which divides according to kinds and does not suppose the same form other nor the other the same (253d1–3). Now, we should not let Theaetetus' hopefulness at their luck occlude our sight. For we have been careful always to remember that the whole task of the *Sophist* is to attempt to see through the sophist's claim to possess the art of purifying souls of ugliness—that is, the art of the noble sophist—and, indeed, to have a godlike omniscience, such as the dialectical science purports to provide. It would be a gross lapse of judgment on our part, then, to entertain too seriously the fact that we have chanced to find the philosopher while still searching for the sophist, especially when all along finding the sophist has been the necessary prelude to even searching for the philosopher. We suspect that it is not to Theaetetus' enterprising reason but to his despairing hope that the dialectical science appeals. Our suspicion only increases when we read the Stranger's description of the capacity this science gives its possessor; this description has long confounded scholars, and distrust is merited when someone who claims to have done the impossible uses exceedingly obscure language. For his part, however, Theaetetus unflinchingly affirms the Stranger's description as "altogether and entirely so" (παντάπασι μὲν οὖν) (253d5–e3). Theaetetus is much too quick to accept the dialectical science as genuine. Let us therefore be more cautious.

Now, the hoped-for dialectical science is introduced as a momentary digression, from which they readily return to the topic at hand, but it immediately becomes clear that it speaks to the concern of the dialogue as a whole. According to the Stranger's rather impenetrable description, "whoever is capable (δυνατὸς) of doing this," namely, of sorting the kinds as the person skilled in the art of letters (γραμματικός) sorts letters, "perceives adequately (ἱκανῶς διαισθάνεται)" the mysterious relationship between looks (ἰδέαι), particulars, and wholes (253d5–e2).[27] The Stranger thus presents the dialectical science as providing us with the capacity to see great things adequately, and so with the capacity to distinguish a distortive apparition from an accurate semblance.[28] That means, by extension, that the dialectical science would address his disagreement with Socrates, as the Stranger indicates when he says it allows not only for the knowing discernment of the mixing of kinds but also for correctly *showing* (δείξειν) which mix (253b11–12). Such showing would have to compensate for the fact that "the eyes of the soul of the many [are] incapable (ἀδύνατα) of being steadfast in looking off (ἀφορῶντα) toward the divine" (254a10–b1). It would thus correct for the ignorance Socrates identified as the intractable cause of the philosopher's distortion as sophist and statesman—indeed, it would free Socrates from the shadowy dream world of which Parmenides once warned him and in which he found himself the day

---

[27] I have restricted the Stranger's highly controversial description of the dialectical science to the basic terms used because my thesis only concerns the acquisition of that science in its most general features. But I agree with Notomi 1999, 235, that the passage is intentionally obscure, though I would attribute it to the fact that the dialectical science appears impossible to acquire, so that one always retains the vestiges of poor sight. For a helpful summary of the leading interpretations of the Stranger's description, see Dorter 1994, 152–54. For a critical reading of these interpretations that situates this important passage within the trilogy as a whole, see Miller 2016, esp. 322–37.

[28] These allusions should suffice to establish the connection between the method of division and the dialectical science, against the skeptical claims of Rosen 1983, 258–59. If only the dialectical science makes us capable of distinguishing among great kinds, then that science must include the Stranger's divisions among great kinds, if indeed he makes them knowingly. See Benardete 2000, 337–38.

before (see Chapter I, Section III, last two paragraphs).[29] Consequently, the dialectical science is the apotheosis of the Theodoran alternative to Socrates, which alternative would practice the most rigorous form of the Stranger's own method of division and its assessment of the true apart from considerations of the good. So, we see that the entire thrust of the dialogue—and, indeed, of the trilogy thus far—drives toward this dialectical science, the possibility of whose acquisition determines whether the philosopher can be distinguished adequately from the sophist and thus whether Socrates, who has just received his indictment, needlessly incurred the Athenians' indignation. Theodorus must be overjoyed—so, too, his modern epigones.

It is at this point, where the Stranger makes the move absolutely necessary to separating the philosopher from the sophist, that we encounter a basic problem that is, I contend, central to the *Sophist* as a whole: the problem of acquiring the dialectical science. Scholars have typically focused on the specific description of the dialectical science rather than its role in the dialogue as a whole.[30]

---

[29] "The *Sophist* and the *Statesman* are two portraits of the Socrates we know, a Socrates who harnesses the quibble in the service of morality. That we do not recognize at once Socrates in his split form testifies to the persuasiveness of Plato, who does not let the seams show. Once, however, Socrates is split, it seems impossible to put him together again, for there is nothing real beyond his double image" (Benardete 2000, 325). Benardete goes on to show how this difficulty is embedded in Socrates "self-portrait" as a midwife in the *Theaetetus*.

[30] The difficulty is quite deep, in fact. For as Gómez-Lobo 1977, 29 notes, "The *communis opinio* is that we are offered there a description of the Method of Division," whose exhaustiveness would have to include the method just practiced. But the essential difficulty is the tension between that description of dialectic (division included) and its actual practice, which is riddled with such error as to show the intractability of avoiding φαντάσματα, that is, of eluding the sophist in the soul (see note 34). Unfortunately, studies of the *Sophist* are primarily concerned with accounting for the method as such, rather than its actual practice, so that the problem of acquiring the dialectical science is never so much as posed. Consider, for example, Notomi 1999, 297–300.

Considering the dialectical science in that larger context, our attention is drawn rather to the difficulty of acquiring the science as the proper difficulty, as the Stranger himself emphasizes their *need* (253b9–c5). That need first emerged from the experience of taking false opinions to be true, of taking an apparition (φάντασμα) to be a semblance (εἰκών). To clear up this confusion, they must first catch the sophist—only then may they arrive at the dialectical science. Yet the conversation began with the observation that the sophist, too, is something great (see 218c5–8). He therefore cannot be seen adequately without first acquiring the capacity to see great things adequately, that is, without first acquiring the dialectical science. It is here that we encounter the aforementioned central difficulty: we cannot catch the sophist without first acquiring the dialectical science, and yet we cannot acquire the dialectical science without first catching the sophist.[31] Just as Socrates' attempt in the *Theaetetus* to distinguish true opinions from false presupposed that this distinction had already been accomplished, so too the attempt to acquire the dialectical science in the *Sophist* presupposes, in its attempt to remove false opinions, that this science has already been acquired.[32] Thus, at the very point when the Stranger appears to have surpassed Socrates, he finds himself mired in the very same problem. That the Stranger knows this all too well is clear from the end of this passage, where he alludes to the present form of the problem. There he says, "Concerning the sophist, surely it's clear that we must not let up until we should see him adequately (ἰκανῶς...θεασώμεθα)" (254b4–6). He thus concludes his discussion of the necessity of acquiring the dialectical science for adequate sight by setting out to see something adequately without that science. To get the science, they need the science; to reach their goal,

---

[31] See *Statesman* 286d8–e4.

[32] Indeed, it is tempting to see in both of these problems very sophisticated epistemological and ontological variants of Socrates' dilemma with Protagoras, namely, that virtue is knowledge, and yet cannot be taught (see *Protagoras* 361a5–c2). See note 10 to the Overture.

they must already be there. The science truly does belong to a god (254a10–b1 with 216b4–c1; compare Parmenides B5).[33]

It turns out, therefore, that the Stranger was right to suspect that the species of spoken images was impassable, and thus that the distinction between apparitions and semblances was something of a dream. And with the peak of the dialogue affirming this suspicion, the *Sophist* as a whole indicates the following horizon to human science. Contrary to Theaetetus' hope, we do not so much construct in speech a semblance (εἰκών) of the beings by means of a dialectical science; rather, we are always on the way to such a semblance and science, which of necessity always recede from view.[34] Philosophy must therefore be understood on the Socratic model, according to which it is a paradoxical combination of the apparition-making and semblance-making arts (φανταστική and εἰκαστική). Of course, we are still at a loss as to the nature of this combination, but there is still much ground left to be covered. Indeed, not until we have returned to the *Theaetetus* will we acquire a sense of what this combination is (see Chapter IV, Sections III and IV). Nevertheless, the *Sophist* does contribute an appreciation of the intimate relationship between being and perplexity, so intimate in fact that perplexity has

---

[33] This difficulty has been subtly present throughout the dialogue, starting with the sophist as something great, but present often in their divisions between great parts or kinds (220b10, 222b2, 229b2, 229c1), in the greatness of the noble sophist's purifications (230d8), and in the greatness of the perplexity they're in (238a2, 238d1), as well as in people, needs, obstacles, etc. (see 230e1, 237a5, 238a1, 243a3, 243d1, 260a6, 261c3). With respect to the divisions in particular, the Stranger's tendency toward revision, which reaches a fever pitch in the *Statesman*, only underscores that, whatever the dialectical science may be, *they* certainly don't have it: the explicit aim of the *Statesman* is to become more dialectical (*Statesman* 285d5–7).

[34] Thus, though I do agree with Notomi 1999, 299, that "the *Sophist* says little about the philosopher, but the dialogue as a whole *shows* something of what the philosopher is" and that "*our* confronting the sophist *within ourselves*" is of the utmost necessity, nevertheless I do not think it is possible "that philosophy can be *secured* and established" (emphasis added).

emerged as necessary to being. Indeed, inasmuch as all spoken images remain finally indistinguishable, one is inclined to understand the Stranger's phrase, "impassable species" (ἄπορον εἶδος), as a profound insight into what being must be in order for there to be human beings, that is, such beings as are essentially puzzled about being (244a4–8 with Aristotle, *Metaphysics* Z.1.1028b2–4).[35]

IV.

As the Stranger returns from discussing the dialectical science, he makes clear that he has rather modest expectations for their attempt—already underway—to solve the perplexities of being and non-being, saying, "if we are not capable (δυνάμεθα) of seizing both being and non-being in all clarity, nevertheless we may come to be not in need of an account, at least (λόγου γε), about them" (254c6–8). He here repeats a comment from when he initiated this attempt prior to his digression on the dialectical science, where he said, "if we should be capable (δυνώμεθα) of seeing neither of the two, then we will examine the account, at least (τὸν γοῦν λόγον), in whatever way we might most plausibly (εὐπρεπέστατα) be able, in this way for both together at the same time" (251a1–3). The Stranger thus returns from the dialectical science with the same modest hopes as before, displaying a willingness to continue the search even *without* the requisite capacity to see or seize great things adequately. Rather, he appears willing to accept in such cases some, *any* account of them: even a spoken image of uncertain veracity will for him suffice, so long as there is something by which his thinking can take its bearings.

---

[35] "The question of the nature of sophist and philosopher, and eventually of statesman, will become entwined with the question of the genera as such and the porosity or impermeability of the boundaries of their mixing or blending or communicating with one another—as if the ignorance of men had a very deep foundation in a theoretical difficulty that leads easily to the confounding of sophist and philosopher" (Cropsey 1995, 70; see, also, 80).

At the same time as he indicates his modest expectations, however, the Stranger enters the section of the dialogue that produces an impressive series of apparently conclusive discoveries: the identification of non-being with the other, the account of false opinion, and the final definition of the sophist. As we will see, an examination of these discoveries reveals their shortcomings, that the uncertain account (λόγος γε) is a deceptive apparition (φάντασμα) and not an accurate semblance (εἰκών). Of course, it should be no wonder that, after having touched upon the inseparability of sophistry from philosophy, the Stranger would combine them himself. For, as Socrates had warned, it is because of the ignorance of those in the city that the philosopher assumes the apparition of the sophist. These apparently conclusive discoveries are not the Stranger's own doctrines but reflections of Theaetetus' defects.

The first putative discovery is the identification of non-being with the other. As the conversation proceeds, they take up the kinds they had been discussing when they encountered the perplexity of being. They refer to them now as the greatest kinds, that is, those that would most be subject to the dialectical science (254b8–d3). They arrive at five kinds—being, motion, rest, same, and other—and conclude that none of them is identical with any of the others (254d4–255e7) and that they mix with each other to differing extents (255e8–257a12). In the course of this examination, they come to observe that by non-being they do not mean something opposite or contrary (ἐναντίον τι) to being but rather something *other*, so that non-being always serves to distinguish the relations among things (257b1–c4). Nothing is said, here, of other possibilities, specifically, of non-being as indicating the non-existence of the subject. On this interpretation, the non-being of a thing consists in its being-other than what it is not. That is, the dog is not a couch, because it is in certain respects *other* than it. Such an interpretation of non-being *promises*, quite powerfully, to help us sort out the sophist's spoken images. The sophist earlier feigned not to know what an image is and even invoked Parmenidean logic to perplex Theaetetus almost into retreat (240c4–7 with 241b4–d9; but consider, also,

240a7–8 and a9–c3, with comment above). Now, however, they stand equipped with a way to show that the sophist's spoken images are distortive apparitions of the relations among things, by showing which kinds mix and which do not. The promise is, therefore, quite powerful indeed.

It is important to understand, however, that the Stranger intends to use a logical identifier—the other—to explain what we today would call an aesthetic phenomenon—the experience of the beautiful (τὸ καλόν). While explaining the nature of the other, the Stranger offers a few examples of how it sets being in opposition to being: the beautiful (τὸ καλόν) is other than the not beautiful, the great (τὸ μέγα) is other than the not great, and the just (τὸ δίκαιον) is other than the not just (257b1–258a10, esp. 257e9–258a6). Likewise, toward the end of the argument he again mentions the beautiful and the great (258a11–c6, esp. b11–c2). Leaving aside for the moment the just, as the Stranger also does, we recognize immediately that it is precisely the difficulty of seeing adequately what is great and beautiful that allows the sophist to deceive us and that necessitated so long a digression on being and non-being. We recall, too, that they had said at that time that images are not, inasmuch as they are not the thing they resemble, but that they also are inasmuch as they are something, that is, something that is of the same sort as the thing imaged in the semblance (240a4–c3). As Theaetetus noticed then but now fails to appreciate, the image is "in its being a semblance" (240b11: εἰκὼν ὄντως). The true being of an image is not to be true being. For this reason, non-being has a special role in the being of images. The image is one thing and so is not all other things; but the image also *is* something among the things it is not, that is, it is what it resembles. If we isolate each of these two modes, the Stranger's logical account works perfectly well: in the former, the image is other than all the others; in the latter, the image is the same (or of the same sort) as something else. What the Stranger's account cannot cope with, however, is both modes together, and it is precisely by doing both together—by both being and not being what the image images—that the image is an image. It is this contradiction, intrinsic to the beautiful itself (αὐτὸ τὸ καλόν), that makes it resistant to rational explication, and so permits the sophist his trickery.

Now, Theaetetus is quite enthused at the discovery, proclaiming that they've identified, as the other, the very thing that the sophist had compelled them to seek, non-being (258b7–8). And, as the Stranger reminds him, they have in so doing confronted Parmenides and even done the unfathomable in overcoming his ironclad logic (258c7–259b8). They have gone where Socrates would not go, and the reward for this daring (τόλμα) is for Theaetetus undeniable. Theaetetus has witnessed first-hand from the Stranger the benefits of didactic parricide. This fact makes Theaetetus' subsequent reaction all the more disappointing, for this unprecedented achievement does not give him the corresponding confidence. As the Stranger turns to confront the sophist's question as to whether speech (λόγος) is among the beings and thus whether their account of the other can be applied thereto, Theaetetus makes clear that he has had about enough of the pursuit. Breaking into an uncharacteristically long speech, he laments that after this obstacle there will perhaps be another and yet another after that, so that "a limit (πέρας), as it seems, in no way will ever appear (φαινήσεταί)" (261a5–b3). In response, the Stranger advises him that "he must be bold, Theaetetus, who is capable (δυνάμενον) of always going forth into what's before him even slightly (καὶ σμικρόν τι)" (261b4–c4). The Stranger here recalls Theaetetus' earlier agreement to continue only on the condition that they be able to seize the sophist "even slightly" (241b4–c6: καὶ κατὰ σμικρὸν). Now, however, he adds that one also needs to be prepared to be thrust backward (261b7: καὶ πάλιν εἰς τοὔπισθεν ἀπωσθείς), that is, to lose one's beloved discoveries upon realizing that what one took for a semblance (ἐικών) was in reality but an apparition (φάντασμα). And it is precisely this that risks occurring in the discussion of false opinion, for there they return to the class of spoken images to see whether their account of non-being can sort out this impassable species (ἄπορον εἶδος). Theaetetus thus leaves the Stranger no choice, for if Theaetetus expresses despair even in the wake of great victory, then what hope can there be for him in the wake of definitive defeat? Faced with his young interlocutor's despair, the Stranger brings the argument to a speedy conclusion, in which he attempts to use his logical solution to the problem of non-being to account for false opinion. The Stranger, we recall, had introduced a digression more than twenty pages long, by substituting non-being for the other in Theaetetus' definition of images, for the purpose, we surmised then and have since observed, of encouraging Theaetetus. We now see, however, that this effort was all for naught.

The Stranger uses their account of non-being as the other to "solve" the problem of false opinion as follows: "when things that are other are spoken as though (ὡς) the same and things that are not as though (ὡς) being, such a synthesis coming to be out of both verbs and nouns in each and every way seems (ἔοικεν) both really and truly (ὄντως τε καὶ ἀληθῶς) to come to be a false speech" (263d1–4). The Stranger here invokes non-being and the other as identical: for x to be y is for x and y to be the same, while for x not to be y is for x and y to be other. A false speech thus occurs when, given that "x is y" is a true opinion, someone states that "x is not y." In this case, one speaks of things that are the same as though (ὡς) they are other. Now, the Stranger's account of false opinion employs the Greek conjunction ὡς, which denotes likeness.[36] Likewise, instead of using the verb "to be," the Stranger uses a form of the verb for seeming—here, ἔοικα—whose substantive is the noun we have translated as "semblance" (εἰκών). This apparently logical solution to the problem of false opinion is, therefore, latently analogical. It is here that we will encounter once again traces of the aforementioned central problem (see Section III, paragraph 9). The language, while analogical, nevertheless suggests that this image is not a distortive

---

[36] Despite the large body of literature on the topic, no scholar of whom I am aware gives attention to this feature of the Stranger's diction. I have profited most from the analysis of Frede 1992.

apparition (φάντασμα) but an accurate semblance (εἰκών). Yet there are good grounds to wonder, as we shall eventually see, whether a whole of parts must, to have parts, be other than itself and, to be a whole, be the same as itself (see Chapter IV, Section III, the central paragraph), so that both the statement "*x* is *y*" and the statement "*x* is not *y*" would somehow be true—so that, to exaggerate somewhat, the statement "*x* both is and is not *y*" would in some sense be true. More simply, this apparently logical solution to the problem of false opinion presupposes that one has arrived at an accurate semblance of being. Every epistemology, in other words, presupposes an ontology. Such a semblance necessarily presupposes, therefore, that those constructing the image have already acquired the dialectical science, which the Stranger and Theatetus have by no means done. The Stranger thus offers, in place of the central philosophic problem of the dialogue, a spurious solution to it, a mere φάντασμα.

Theaetetus detects none of this. In one respect, his acceptance is not surprising, since what he longs for is a final escape from the sophist, and the Stranger intends his account to keep Theaetetus, already inclined to give up, from getting still further discouraged (see 261a5–c5, 264b6–11). But in another respect, he would do well to attend to the fact that the escape he gets is an apparition (φάντασμα). For just the day before Socrates had rebuked him for using the phrase "truly false" (ἀληθῶς ψευδῆ) during their discussion of false opinion (*Theaetetus* 189b12–d6). It is therefore peculiar that the Stranger's use of "both really and truly" (ὄντως τε καὶ ἀληθῶς) alongside "false speech" (λόγος ψευδής) doesn't jog his memory. But perhaps this is testimony of how Theaetetus' relief at finally being rid of the sophist shades his memory and judgment. He is perhaps all too happy to accept the final definition of the sophist, which assigns to him an art of making apparitions (φανταστική), despite the fact that "spoken images" remains an "impassable species" (ἄπορον εἶδος) (268c8–d5). Consequently, the three positive results after the aporetic peak of the dialogue in the digression on the dialectical science—the identification of non-being with the other, the account of false opinion, and the final definition of the sophist—are the Stranger's distortive apparitions, constructed to satisfy Theaetetus' longing for a solution, while offering something to his skepticism and curiosity.[37] As it now stands, of course, the former wins out in the battle over Theaetetus' soul. The Stranger had hoped to use Theaetetus' deference to him to undermine itself by having him imitate his didactic patricide of Parmenides. Now, however, we see that Theaetetus will object only to further problems, not to attractive but spurious solutions. His dominating desire is, at this point, to have leave of the conversation.

Accordingly, the dialogue never adequately addresses the perspective from which it began, that of the youth enchanted by the sophist's teaching but suspicious of his moral rectitude. The ever-increasing perplexities that the sophist has cast before Theaetetus have dulled for him the charm of the sophist's enchantment. If any headway is to be made in the problem of Socrates, it will not be with Theaetetus. We must therefore return to the basic issue that emerged with the introduction of the noble sophist, where refutation corrected the paternal, merely admonitory education offered by the city through a purification of the soul's ugly or shameful ignorance (229e1–230e5). We now see that it is not by dispelling the sophist's speeches as distortions—as simply an analogical or, worse, logical problem—but by allowing our enchantment, with all its moral and political connotations, to arouse our curiosity that we come to appreciate the sophist's significance for the problem of Socrates. Without such enchantment, Theaetetus remains completely under the sway of the unacknowledged moral-political standard to which he (and Theodorus) appear to hold philosophy. The argument does not account for the action, in which it is found and which it is meant to explain. Had it attempted to, it would have asked

---

[37] The most thorough examination of the Stranger's speeches in light of the distinction between φανταστική and εἰκαστική is Benardete 2000, 323–53. On the Stranger as no less φαῦλος in speeches than Socrates, see Howland 1998, 211–12, who notes that the Stranger's mixture of being and non-being is as impure as Socrates' mixture of knowledge and ignorance in the *Theaetetus*.

whether the distinction between knowledge and ignorance should be understood in light of the distinction between the beautiful and the ugly, whether it distorted philosophy to demand that it be pure and purifying. The attempt to ascend to the true in absence of the good appears to have been something of a beautiful fiction. What they must consider, therefore, is whether philosophy can purge all citizens of their ignorance, as this moral-political standard would have it. They must examine the knowing statesman, precisely the inquiry taken up in the sequel, the *Statesman*.

One can say, therefore, that the *Sophist* has attempted to reduce τὸ καλόν, a Greek term varied in meaning and thus essentially contentious, simply to the analogical (or so-called aesthetic) meaning of the beautiful, over and against its more political meaning as the noble. When the Stranger gave examples of how the other separates being from being, he mentioned the great, the beautiful, and the just, whose combination would appear to restrict the meaning of τὸ καλόν to the noble; but when he repeated this list he dropped the just (257e9–258a6, b11–c2). Likewise, when the Stranger and Theaetetus listed the sophist's areas of expertise, the Stranger asked, "But what, in turn, about laws and all the political things, do [sophists] not promise to make [their students] disputatious [about these]?" Theaetetus pregnantly responded, "Well, no one would converse with them, in a word, if they didn't promise this!" (232d1–4)[38] The sophist's most immediate apparition is not so much of the philosopher as it is of the statesman—indeed, of the divinely competent statesman. To investigate the sophist adequately, then, one must proceed rather through the sophist's apparition as a statesman. The *Statesman* does just that in its latter portion, where the Stranger sets as their task separating the scientific statesman from all the partners in other regimes—those he calls the greatest sorcerers and charlatans of all the sophists and the most experienced in this art (*Statesman* 267c5–268d4, 291a1–c8, 303b8–c7, esp. 291c3–4 with 303b8–

---

[38] Consider, too, 225c7–10 and 268b1–c4.

c5). Just as the Stranger and Theaetetus stumbled across the philosopher during their search for the sophist, the Stranger and Young Socrates will stumble across the sophist during their search for the statesman. Will they also thereby stumble across the philosopher?[39] In any case, the *Sophist* really and truly was a false start, as their implicit understanding of the sophist was a distortion. If there is a way out of the problem of Socrates, it is to be found in an examination of the statesman and it is to be pursued without Theaetetus. It is this way that the Stranger explores in the sequel.

---

[39] See Chapter III, Section II, tenth paragraph.

III

STATESMAN

I.

In response to the gratitude Socrates expresses to Theodorus for introducing him to Theaetetus and the Stranger, Theodorus remarks that his gratitude will triple once they have together brought to light both the statesman and the philosopher (257a1–5).[1] Theodorus' response contains two errors: he sees neither the derivative worth of the sophist nor Theaetetus' aversion to enduring his tricks any longer (257c5–7). But as we have come to understand it, the sophist is parasitic not primarily on the philosopher but on the statesman, so that the turn to the latter constitutes the proper starting point for the understanding of all three. The *Statesman* makes this adjustment and thus delivers on the Stranger's warning to Theaetetus that one must be prepared not just for minor progress but even for regress (*Sophist* 261b4–c4). The *Statesman* is the Stranger's second sailing on his Theodoran attempt to solve the problem of Socrates. The *Sophist*'s worth is as derivative as that of the sophist himself. The *Statesman*, we hope, will redeem the *Sophist*'s inquiry by correcting for its erroneous beginning point. The goal of the *Sophist* has *not*, therefore, been set aside with the *Statesman* but incorporated into

---

[1] Unless noted otherwise, all references in this chapter are to the *Statesman*.

it.[2] The Stranger thus reorients the conversation by replacing Theaetetus, beleaguered by the proliferating perplexities, with Young Socrates, whose combination of eagerness and curiosity allow the Stranger to put the conversation on its proper path.[3]

The Stranger incorporates the goal of the *Sophist* into that of the *Statesman* through the increasing attention paid to methodological concerns. The goal the Stranger initially sets for himself and Young Socrates is to find the statesman (258b1–3). More specifically, he says he wishes to discover the distinct look (ἰδέα) of his science, such that all other sciences are grouped into a single species (εἶδος) (258c3–7). The Stranger thus proposes they discover what we will call an *epistemic heterogeneity*, according to which the nature of knowledge opposes one science to all the rest.[4] During the first of the dialogue's two stages (258b2–287b3), the Stranger attempts to show Young Socrates the difficulty of attaining this goal, as their repeated errors and confusions compel them to take a number of methodological digressions recalling the *Sophist* (262a3–263c3,

---

[2] "If...the *Statesman*, in defining the statesman, defines the sophist as well, the *Sophist* must be the *phantasma* of the *eikōn* the *Statesman* is" (Benardete 2000, 373).

[3] But as we will see, Young Socrates' character will pose its own obstacles, distinctive from and even complementary to those posed by Theaetetus'. The Stranger is thus able to make progress over the *Sophist* in the *Statesman*, while pointing to the fact that it is not enough to be more eager than Theaetetus to forge through the problem of Socrates. Theaetetus' despair, it will turn out, is not without its instructive element.

[4] The situation is somewhat more complicated, as the Stranger then immediately refers to the ἰδέα of statecraft and the εἶδος of the other sciences as *two* εἴδη (258c3–7). Following Davis and Benardete on the *Republic*, we might distinguish between εἶδος and ἰδέα according to the distinction between the question, "What is *x*?", and a putative answer to that question (see Davis 2018b, 119, Benardete 1989, 215–16). If that distinction applies here, then the Stranger would suggest that the questionable being of the other sciences would, by virtue of being other than statecraft, undermine any putative definition of statecraft. This would be to affirm Socrates' suggestion that one cannot know anything before knowing what science is (*Theaetetus* 196e2–7).

277d1–278e12, 283b1–287b3), in addition to noticing the parallels between the hunt for the sophist and the search for the statesman (266d4–11, 284b4–c6 with 286b3–c5). Reflecting on these problems, the Stranger proposes that they use one of the other sciences as a model or paradigm (παράδειγμα), off of which they can construct an image of statecraft. But here we encounter a difficulty. How, we wonder, can they find the unique look of statecraft by means of a model? Wouldn't using another science as a model risk imposing upon statecraft those features common to the model's species, foreign as it is to statecraft's look? Thus, about halfway through, the Stranger revises the goal, asking Young Socrates, "But what about our present search for the statesman? Did we put it forward (προβέβληται) for the sake of this [man] himself more than [for the sake of] becoming more dialectical (διαλεκτικωτέροις) in all things?" (285d5–7) Young Socrates affirms that this is clearly the case (285d8). So, now that the Stranger's method is at odds with the epistemic heterogeneity of his goal, he remarks that the search for the statesman is necessary to the goal of becoming more dialectical.[5] To understand the place of the *Statesman* within the trilogy, therefore, we will first have to consider how the search for the statesman generates the Stranger's methodological digressions and how those digressions incorporate themes from the *Sophist* (Section II).

However questionable their method may be, nevertheless the Stranger and Young Socrates attempt to apply the model of weaving to statecraft in the dialogue's second stage (287b4–311c10). The conversation thereafter proceeds much more smoothly, as they follow the plan provided by the model almost entirely without disruption. They do, however, take one digression that deviates from the model—namely, on law, which proves necessary to statecraft while falling short of the scientific standard of precision. It seems, then,

---

[5] For this reason we should not take the Stranger to mean, as some have, that the search for the statesman is merely incidental to the goal of becoming more dialectical, as though another subject could simply replace the statesman with no impact on that goal. This is too Theodoran, just as it would be to take Young Socrates also to be incidental and thus replaceable.

that it is law that gives statecraft its unique look. For the necessary imprecision of law makes the notion of the doctor or pilot legislating utterly strange (ἄτοπα); indeed, such legislation would appear destructive of the various arts' benefits, succeeding only in rendering still more difficult our already difficult lives (297e8–298e3). Despite this departure from the model, however, Young Socrates will fail to appreciate statecraft's uniqueness, being far too taken with the relevance of the model to demand a further inquiry into the element of statecraft at odds with the model: law, *inviolable* law, on pains of the greatest of punishments (297d4–e5). In his eagerness, he will stop the dialogue short, missing thereby the core of scientific statecraft (Section III). This error is quite severe, as the core of statecraft resembles Socratic refutation and so promises to elucidate the relation between the sophist, statesman, and philosopher. Robbing us of this inquiry, the *Statesman* would thus fail to find the statesman, if not also to make us more dialectical. It would appear, then, to end in tragedy, just as the *Theaetetus* and *Sophist* before it. But precisely because these latter two tragedies concern the *critique* of Socrates, the action of their argument serves as a *modus tollens* on the possibility of a scientific alternative to Socratic political philosophy (Section IV). In this way, they set the stage for our return to the *Theaetetus* as the missing *Philosopher*—as Socrates' written testament as to why he had to be misunderstood.

II.

The first and second stages of the argument differ most manifestly with respect to the number of mistakes made and digressions taken. In the course of the first part, the Stranger pauses occasionally to reflect on their method—namely, on the manner of division (262a3–263c3), on the necessity of thinking through models (277d1–278e12), and on the criterion by which one should praise or blame the length of a speech (283b1–287b3). The culmination of these digressions is the Stranger's advice to Young Socrates that the method, the pursuit or way (μέθοδος), may occasionally entail a byway (περίοδος) (286d4–287a6). Thus, in the first stage the Stranger prepares Young Socrates to welcome such digressive extensions in the argument as had discouraged Theaetetus. The Stranger's advice is all the more important, again, as he wants to use another science, different from statecraft, as a model for it, hoping thereby to find the distinct look (ἰδέα) of the science of statecraft, such that all the other arts and sciences can be grouped into a single species (εἶδος) (258c3–7). The tension between his goal and his proposed method of attaining that goal suggests that the way (μέθοδος) to the statesman *entails* a deviation from itself (περίοδος).

It is not without justification that the Stranger expects from Young Socrates an eagerness not found in Theaetetus. Though Theaetetus had been unwilling to put himself on a par with the Stranger, Young Socrates' deference does not prevent him from agreeing that the work (τὸ ἔργον) is theirs together (258c3–d3, *Sophist* 234d2–e7). In line with this eagerness outside his element, Young Socrates readily agrees to extend the model of arithmetic to statecraft by assigning to the statesman a wholly cognitive science; indeed, so cognitive is this science that its bearer earns the title of statesman regardless of what he rules and even of whether he rules at all (258d4–259d6). That this extension is overly eager and thus ignores the non-cognitive component of statecraft is immediately clear when the Stranger speaks not just of the intelligence of the statesman's soul but of its strength, as well (259c8: τὴν τῆς ψυχῆς σύνεσιν καὶ ῥώμην). Likewise, in the next division the statesman is assigned an injunctive art, in that he gives orders to others, as opposed to the more completely cognitive critical art (κριτική) belonging, for example, to the logistician, in his cognition of number, or to an observer (θεατής) (259d7–260c5).[6] Whereas Theaetetus was an isolationist mathematician, restricting himself to it and akin

---

[6] I owe these observations on the first two divisions, as well as the importance of the herald or prophet in connection to the digression on law, to Seth Appelbaum.

studies while declaring universal ignorance about the sorts of things Socrates customarily discusses, Young Socrates is an imperialist mathematician, willing to develop a wholly scientific conception of statecraft through a quasi-Cartesian extension of the model of mathematics—through the development of a methodology, if you will. But the equal applicability of mathematics to the various arts and sciences requires an epistemic homogeneity at cross-purposes with the Stranger's attempt to discover the unique look of statecraft, that is, to discover an epistemic heterogeneity. Young Socrates thus differs from Theaetetus primarily in that his eagerness suggests a latent—but so far only latent—attraction to methodology.

That the extension of mathematics to other sciences uses it as a *model* suggests that the justification for this extension is not logical but analogical—that it relies on imagery rather than argument. Methodology, it seems, has a methodologically questionable basis. What we lose in that analogy is, again, the unscientific component to statecraft—what the Stranger calls strength (ῥώμη) of soul but we today might call charisma. Young Socrates' eagerness, however, leads him to pass over this component. But why? Recalling the *Sophist*, the Stranger remarks that, just as the retailer differed from the "self-seller" (αὐτοπώλης), so too does the herald differ from "the one issuing injunctions of his own" (αὐτεπιτάκτης), namely, as what derives from another (ἀλλοτριότης) differs from what is one's own (260c6–261a3). The self-enjoiner (αὐτεπιτάκτης) preserves for himself what the self-seller (αὐτοπώλης) commodified for another, and so replaces the self-selling of prostitution with a giving of injunctions that comes only from within—with what we might call a mixture of authenticity and autonomy. In this way, the scientific statesman possesses a self-directedness not enjoyed by the herald, the prophet, and the religious interpreter; he thus replaces god (260d11–261a1). It is scientific pride, then, that leads Young Socrates to pass over the unscientific component of statecraft and its theological corollaries. But of what is this proud scientist so proud? After they agree that the statesman's injunctions are for the sake of the coming into being of living beings and, specifically, a herd of living beings, the Stranger asks Young Socrates which herd-animal the statesman commands, enjoining the young man to divide the double in half, that is, into two equal units (261a2–262a2). Young Socrates accepts the challenge, noting his own eagerness (προθυμήσομαι), but disobeys the Stranger's arithmetical stricture: instead of dividing herd-nurture in half, he divides it lopsidedly into the nurture of human beings and that of all other herd-animals (262a3–4). As has been noted, Young Socrates' division is based in human pride.[7] More exactly, his eagerness goes more to his pride in having the (or an) answer than to the evenness of his division.[8] In either case, we see to what sort of pride the beautiful promise of methodology appeals: it is a pride in man's ability to answer precisely and to do so quickly.

The Stranger thus takes his first methodological digression as a correction of Young Socrates' "most eager and most manly dividing" (262a5–6). This digression has the effect of making explicit or active Young Socrates' latent attraction to methodology. The Stranger notices in Young Socrates' separation of man from all other animals a general tendency in thinking, in which one kind (γένος) is separated from all other kinds (γένη); those kinds (γένη) are then treated erroneously as constituting a single kind (γένος), when in fact they are "limitless, immiscible, and lacking in consonance" (262a6–263a1). The Stranger uses the example of how the Greeks proudly divide the human race (γένος) by grouping themselves as being of one descent (γένος), with all other peoples constituting the spurious kind (γένος) of barbarians. In reality, this "kind" comprises a number of descents or races (γένη), so that they have divided the human race into parts (μέρη) rather than kinds (γένη). Likewise, another intelligent animal (φρόνιμόν...τι ζῷον ἕτερον), like a crane, might call all other animals beasts, man included (263d3–e2; see Herodotus, *Histories* 2.158.5). A more natural and less prideful

---

[7] See, for example, Howland 1998, 234, 244; Strauss 1987, 71.
[8] Perhaps, however, Young Socrates believes that man is so great as to be equal in worth to all other animals combined. See *Statesman* 257a1–b8.

division of the human race would, the Stranger argues, separate male from female. For that distinction appeals to the natural joint (διαφυή) rather than human hubris (see 259d10–11). So the Stranger argues, at least. We, of course, find it peculiar to compare Young Socrates' division of animals into human beings and beasts to the tendency of the Greeks to distinguish all human beings into Greeks and barbarians.[9] The Stranger relies on the ambiguous meaning of γένος as both descent and kind, scrupulously avoiding any mention of species or form (εἶδος), even when it would have been more appropriate to his point. Had he spoken otherwise, however, he would have exposed the fact that man has both a descent (γένος) and a species (εἶδος), while Greek seems only to be a descent (γένος)—at least at first glance. That is, "the Greeks," as it were, would have to be a model imaging a species or form (εἶδος) of human being rather than naming but another descent of human beings (see Herodotus, *Histories* 2.2 with 3.38).

That the Stranger so easily persuades Young Socrates of the arbitrariness of his division suggests that his use of "beast" is moral rather than scientific—that he has pride in being the intelligent animal (ζῷον φρόνιμον). The Stranger's "correction," then, appears to pit this pride against itself. That is, by suppressing the difference between descent (γένος) and species (εἶδος), the Stranger draws out Young Socrates' curiosity: Young Socrates not only welcomes the digression but wants to extend it so as to understand how "to recognize more vividly kind and part" (263a2–4). By so exploiting the youth's curiosity, the Stranger develops his pride in precision into an attraction to methodology, in the hopes, we surmise, of leading him to more serious reflection on thinking. Methodology, of course, is still too proud, in that its attempt at formalizing all thinking assumes an epistemic homogeneity, against the heterogeneity necessary to the Stranger's purpose of discovering the unique look of

---

[9] A wolf-pup placed among dogs would not thereby become as philanthropic, while Oedipus blended in seamlessly with his adoptive home. Compare Exodus 2:1–14.

statecraft. Will the Stranger be successful in converting Young Socrates' pride in precision into an appreciation of statecraft's uniqueness? We recall that the Stranger had attempted to use Theaetetus' deference to undermine itself by making deference entail didactic parricide, that is, by making deference entail defiance. Theaetetus, however, proved willing to defy the Stranger only to escape the conversation, not to undo their apparent progress. Will Young Socrates' pride in precision lead him to make the reverse error? Will it incline him to accept the model of weaving at face value, and so miss what is distinctive about statecraft? Or will his curiosity overpower his pride, and so welcome deviation from the pre-set path of methodology?

This challenge proves formidable. As he completes the divisions, the Stranger takes great pains to temper the youth's pride through an overwhelming series of mistakes, revisions, and more.[10]

---

[10] When the Stranger returns to their divisions, he identifies a further mistake, namely, that, prior to their division of the nurturing of herds, they had left out the distinction been the savage and domesticated or tame (263e7). After locating statecraft within animal-nurture, he explains that they ought not to have jumped immediately to herding animals but rather first distinguished them into the savage and the domesticated or tame, with the herding to be found among the latter (263e9–264a7). Though Young Socrates admits the digression has slowed them down, he is nevertheless delighted by where it has taken them (264a8–b6). The Stranger will have to do more to temper his excessive eagerness. The Stranger then points to a short and a long way to finish their divisions; though this might have deterred Theaetetus, with Young Socrates it appears intended to magnify his curiosity into gluttony, as he requests that they take both and then expresses gratitude upon completion (265a1–b1, 267a1–3). The Stranger must therefore go further, as indeed he does. By rejecting Young Socrates' earlier, most eager, and most manly division, they discover that the statesman's closest kin is the swineherd (266b10–d11). Like Diogenes in his famous joke, Young Socrates also finds this humbling result strange and laughable (266c7, d3), agreeing as well that they likely spoke correctly when, in the *Sophist*, they noted the method's indifference to honor (266d11; see *Sophist* 226e8–227c6). Nevertheless, he is delighted that they have achieved their stated goal, affirming the conclusion as altogether and entirely so (267c4: παντάπασι μὲν οὖν).

Young Socrates, however, responds only with delight and gluttony. Indeed, far from second-guessing their now completed definition, he proclaims that they have achieved their stated goal, affirming the conclusion as altogether and entirely so (267c4: παντάπασι μὲν οὖν). Whereas Theaetetus was inclined to believe that thinking about what knowledge is was doomed to opacity, Young Socrates believes that he has achieved perfect clarity. With Theaetetus, the Stranger feigned conclusiveness; thus, with Young Socrates he must appear exceedingly uncertain (see Section IV). Seizing upon Young Socrates' "altogether and entirely" (παντάπασι), the Stranger asks whether they've spoken truly (ἀληθῶς...εἴρηκας), in claiming to have spoken altogether and entirely sufficiently (τὸ παντάπασιν ἱκανῶς εἰρῆσθαι), or rather they haven't accomplished their work altogether and entirely perfectly (οὐ μὴν παντάπασί γε τελέως ἀπειργάσθαι) (267c5–d2). Ever eager, Young Socrates insists that the Stranger speak (267d3). The Stranger says, "I will attempt for myself to clarify for the two of us still more this very thing that I am now thinking through" (267d4–5: ἐγὼ νῷν πειράσομαι τοῦτ' αὐτὸ ὃ διανοοῦμαι νῦν ἔτι μᾶλλον δηλῶσαι).[11] By using such highly reflexive and uncertain language, the Stranger emphasizes the opacity of their path or way (μέθοδος) to the statesman.[12] Though sure that an error has occurred, he is unsure (or feigns he is

---

[11] For the strangeness of the language here, compare the simpler phrase at *Alcibiades* 104e5–6. See, also, the following note.

[12] The Stranger's statement is doubly reflexive, with the middle voice of πειράσομαι indicating that the attempt is for himself and the dative dual νῷν indicating that he attempts or clarifies for both of them together. That is, the Stranger acts as though he himself is in the dark about what he is thinking, as though he himself is learning as he teaches Young Socrates—indeed, he opts for διανοέω over ἐννοέω. Still more, it is difficult to know whether νῦν ἔτι μᾶλλον goes with διανοοῦμαι or δηλῶσαι, whether these adverbs are to be split, and—if so—which of them go(es) with which verb. Is the Stranger thinking now still more or will he clarify now still more? Or is he thinking now and will clarify still more, or is he thinking now still and will clarify more? These possibilities all fall on a spectrum, according to which thinking and communicating work not sequentially but simultaneously.

unsure) as to what exactly it is. Through the example of his conduct, the Stranger impresses upon Young Socrates the unmethodological side to thinking—how to be on one's way thinking something through is to be not altogether sure of what it is. Indeed, if this weren't the case, thinking either wouldn't be possible or would be altogether superfluous.[13] Rather, it must always reside between simple obscurity and simple clarity, if it is to be what it is (see *Theaetetus* 188a1–6 with 210b6–7).

Despite the Stranger's uncertainty, Young Socrates' questions remain insistent, always urging his elder to explain himself further or to move on to the next point (267d6, e3, 6, 268a5). When Theaetetus responded to the Stranger's altogether obscure description of the dialectical science with an "altogether and entirely so" (παντάπασι μὲν οὖν) of his own, the Stranger made no effort to question the youth's certainty (*Sophist* 253e3). Whereas Theaetetus affirmed that they stand in need of the dialectical science more than anything else, Young Socrates affirms their conclusions as though they already have that science. Unlike other herders, the Stranger continues, the statesman finds his title as herdsman and nurse of the human herd under dispute by doctors, trainers, farmers, and so on (267e1–268b8). Because the statesman's work is shared, they have yet to accomplish their own work with precision (ἀπειργασμένοι... δι' ἀκριβείας): they must first separate him from these disputants pure and alone (καθαρὸν μόνον) (268b9–d1). Despite his claims to the contrary, then, the Stranger's method appears to consider the true as bound up with the good in some fashion or another, that is, according the Socratic understanding as opposed to the Theodoran—the true without the good—or the Protagorean—the good

---

[13] Cropsey sees this problem as intrinsic to the Stranger's method as such: "The long and tedious process of diremption seems to have as its aim the refinement of an indistinct opinion to the state of precise knowledge" (Cropsey 1995, 112).

without the true (see 266d4–11).[14] In addition, toward the end of separating the statesman from his disputants, the Stranger proposes the playful approach of making use of a long part of a great myth, only thereafter returning to their previous method of dividing (268d8–e7). That is, the Stranger explicitly deviates from the sort of mathematically precise divisions that he had insisted upon so firmly just moments ago. Setting that aside for now, we note that their new, more playful approach involves reconstructing out of hearsay and fragmentary evidence—such tatters and echoes as remain after the ravages of time—a cosmic experience or occurrence (πάθος) from long ago (268e8–269c3). It is unclear what purpose this cosmic occurrence is to play in their search for the statesman, as the Stranger promises no fewer than seven times in five pages that he will soon get to the point (269b9–c1, 270b3–5, 271e2–5, 272d4–6, 273e4–6, 274b1–2, d8–e3). Initially, the Stranger's postponement irritates Young Socrates, whose eagerness tends toward impatience as he again urges the Stranger forward (268e7, 269c3, d4). But Young Socrates soon finds the story intriguing, a semblance of reality (270b1–2: φαίνεται...εἰκότως εἰρῆσθαι, c3: ἔοικε, 6: καὶ τοῦτο εἰκός, d5). Eventually, his curiosity supersedes his urgency, as his questions push the Stranger still further off his planned course and onto a digression (271a3–4, c3–7). The Stranger thus uses Young Socrates' gluttony to modify his eagerness, in the hopes, it appears, of developing it into open curiosity. In this way, he prepares the youth for his later methodological warning that the way (μέθοδος) might require a byway (περίοδος).

---

[14] This opposition between Theodorus and Protagoras trickles down to their ways of life: "Protagoras's anti-theoretical stance rules out the achievement not only of wisdom or knowledge but also of political goods such as justice and virtue, while Theodorus's aloofness from the political community guarantees that he will lack self-knowledge as well as any practical alternative to the politics of sophistry. Philosophy and politics fall apart from each other in the characters of Theodorus and Protagoras, and both of these spheres are thereby corrupted" (Howland 1998, 51).

The specific experience or occurrence that the Stranger wants to examine concerns a purported change of direction in the rotations or circuits (περίοδοι) of the cosmos. According to the myth, the cosmos rotates in two directions, depending on whether the god conducts (συμποδηγεῖ: literally, "compedes") it along its way (πορευόμενον) and aids it in turning (συγκυκλεῖ) or at another time lets it go, at which point the natural necessity (ἐξ ἀνάγκης ἔμφυτον) of turning in the other direction takes over (269c4–d3). The mythic tradition—the echoes, as it were, of the original experience or occurrence—has named the former rotation the age of Kronos, while the present is referred to as the age of Zeus (269a7–8, 271b9–c2, 272b1–3, 274c5–d2). We note, for later, that the Stranger implies that his adherence to Zeus' law of guest-friendship (ξενία) was merely *pro forma*. That aside, the cause (αἴτιον) of this reversal is the corporeal form (σωματοειδές) of the cosmos, intrinsic to its original nature (φύσις) (273a1–b7). As the cosmos proceeded in the circuit or rotation (περίοδος) opposite to the present one, the difficulties and injustices (χαλεπὰ καὶ ἄδικα), the worthless things (φλαῦρα), were quite small in comparison with the beautiful (καλά) and good things (ἀγαθά), which were great (μεγάλα) (273b7–c5). But with the god having let the cosmos go, the experience or occurrence of its original disharmony (τὸ τῆς παλαιᾶς ἀναρμοστίας πάθος) came to dominate, so that the cosmos found itself to be in perplexities (ἐν ἀπορίαις ὄντα)—in a limitless sea of dissimilarities, as it were—until the god set it aright again (273c6–e4; compare *Parmenides* 164b5–165e1). The specific experience or occurrence (πάθος), therefore, that the Stranger seeks to elucidate is that of the perplexities innate to the cosmos and, indeed, to being itself. The Stranger thus explicitly imports the ontology that was implicit in the *Sophist*. Significantly, however, he does so by adapting it to a cosmology.

The significance of this adaptation is that it involves a shift from the primary meaning that the term ἀπορία had in the *Sophist*, a shift similar to the shift in the meaning of τὸ καλόν from "the beautiful" to "the noble" (see Chapter II, Section IV). Whereas in the *Sophist* ἀπορία almost always meant "perplexity," in the *Statesman* its meaning drifts closer to "being without resource or recourse." It is the essential resourcelessness of the human condition, then, that the Stranger seeks to elucidate through his myth of the cosmic experience or occurrence. Without the god's provision or guidance, the Stranger explains, all the animals harsh in nature (χαλεπὰ τὰς φύσεις) grew wild (ἀπαγριωθέντων; consider *Sophist* 217d8–218a1), against which these now unguarded (ἀφύλακτοι) human beings had no devices (ἀμήχανοι) or arts (ἄτεχνοι), not knowing how to provide (πορίζεσθαι...οὐκ ἐπιστάμενοί) for themselves the nourishment that in the prior circuits had come forth spontaneously (αὐτομάτης) (274b5–c4). Confronted by such a situation, man notices that he lives in the midst of great ἀπορίαι, great difficulties or problems, great resourcelessness or perplexities (ἐν μεγάλαις ἀπορίαις)—that is, he experiences however crudely the ontology of the *Sophist*—and so seeks to guard himself with devices, arts, and sciences of provision. That the arts and sciences offer provision in this state of being provisionless appears to make them essentially practical.[15] But if to be human is to be in the midst of great resourcelessness, that is, to dwell among perplexities and problems (ἀπορίαι), can statecraft actually guard against all the difficulties the cosmos throws our way? And if there were still perplexities to ponder despite all our needs being provided for, would not that last

---

[15] The keystone of this arrangement of the sciences would, we surmise, be the dialectical science: though its primary purpose was theoretical—that is, to see, perceive, or grasp the great things sufficiently—still its secondary purpose was practical, that is, to show these things to another and thereby purge him of false opinions (*Sophist* 253b11–12). Indeed, the statesman will finally be said to instill in the souls of the citizens a true opinion that really is (ὄντως οὖσαν) about the beautiful, just, and good things, and the things contrary to these (309c1–9). Likewise, the Stranger will soon argue that the statesman possesses a science akin to that of weaving, whose twin actions are examples of separation (διακρίνεσθαι) and combination (συγκρίνεσθαι), that is, the two elements of dialectics (διαλέγεσθαι or διαλεκτική) (282b1–283a9, esp. 282b2).

need, that of the dialectical science, perhaps the greatest science, remain (*Sophist* 253c4–5)? Or would we never seek that science, since no need would compel us (τὸ μηδεμίαν αὐτοὺς χρείαν... ἀναγκάζειν) to such a search (274c3–4)?

Thanks to Young Socrates' newly piqued curiosity, the Stranger touches upon this question during a brief digression, in which he is ambivalent about whether men in the age of Kronos merely grazed like cattle or rather philosophized (272b1–d4). This is the sole mention of philosophy in the *Statesman* outside of the prologue (272c1–2; 257a5, c1). If, as the Stranger noted, the difference between the age of Kronos and that of Zeus is, with respect to the perplexities or problems (ἀπορίαι), a difference of degree and not a difference in kind, then philosophy should, strictly speaking, be possible in this prior age. But if it is the *experience* of need that compels us, as the Stranger says, to take seriously these problems, then in the age of Kronos philosophy may have been possible without ever having been actual. Philosophy would never actually *be*, unless the city also is: philosophy would only actually *be* as political philosophy.[16] The Stranger's description of the practice of philosophy in the age of Kronos appears to confirm this point. Should such men have philosophized, they would have associated both with the animals and with one another so as to learn through inquiry from every nature whether a certain one, having some private capacity or power, perceives something different from the rest (272c1–4). That is, they would have investigated Protagoras' claim, whether man is the measure of all things and whether what appears for each man also *is* for him.[17] Does the problem of the philosopher and the sophist persist even in absence of the city? One is tempted to understand philosophy so characterized as a caricature of the conversations in the *Theaetetus* and *Sophist*, which construed the problem of the sophist

---

[16] On necessity and the provocation to philosophy, see Howland 1998, 265.

[17] Howland also finds the description of philosophy here to be peculiarly circumscribed, though for somewhat different reasons (Howland 1998, 263–64).

in partial abstraction from the city: in both, the philosopher was depicted as wholly free.[18] But perhaps this brief digression could instead be understood as a profound statement on the possibility of philosophy, namely, that no matter how changed human nature may be, even should generation be reversed and lacking in sexual reproduction, nevertheless so long as a corporeal being is intelligent and corporeal nature is flawed, philosophy is indeed possible (compare Aristotle, *Metaphysics* α.2.994a25–b3).

Be that as it may, the Stranger has brought the now curious Young Socrates to a question they do not and likely even cannot answer. And he connects it to such an understanding of the world as is not conducive to precision, that is, as is better expressed through a myth than through the Stranger's quasi-mathematical divisions. It is perhaps for this reason, then, that the Stranger makes their return to the second definition of the statesman so rocky. As he resumes the definition, the Stranger again notes their mistake but adds that they were additionally mistaken about the severity of their mistake; oddly, however, the Stranger is ambivalent about whether it was more or less severe than they had initially thought (274d8–e8).[19] As it stands, their statesman lays claim to a divine power, and thus finds his claim to tending the human herd under dispute (275a8–c8). They must, therefore, begin from something common to all herders—namely, tending or caring—and then specify what and how the statesman tends (275c9–e9). As for *what* the

---

[18] In support of this possibility, consider the myth in light of *Theaetetus* 161c2–d1.

[19] Rather, it seems to be both, depending on context (*contra* Howland 1998, 166): on the one hand, the lack of specificity they've given the statesman's art is easily corrected through more precise specification; on the other hand, however, it also means that they've attributed to the statesman much too broad capabilities—indeed, so broad that the statesman appears to possess the cosmic governance of a Kronos (274e9–275a7; see 268c5–11). This specification, then, serves to pare down Young Socrates' pride, which had classified the statesman as an αὐτεπιτάκτης, giving him a self-directedness above the herald or prophet and so on the level of a god.

statesman tends, they need only use the prior divisions of animals, by which they arrived at man; it is rather by specifying *how* he tends man that they can separate the statesman from the disputants (276a1–b7). Toward this end, they make but one distinction, namely, that no other artisan would be willing to claim it cares for all of the human community together (276b8–c2). Young Socrates affirms the distinction as correctly spoken (276c3: λέγεις ὀρθῶς). His easy affirmation is striking, in that they drew out a long myth as a correction, only to complete the job with a single distinction. Still more striking is that, prior to the myth, Young Socrates had also affirmed the opposite claim as "correctly spoken" (see 267e7–268a5, esp. a5: οὐκοῦν ὀρθῶς ἂν λέγοιεν). As though to emphasize for Young Socrates the need for great care, the Stranger follows his hasty assent with the revelation of a second mistake, namely, their failure to distinguish the statesman from the tyrant in terms of whether those they rule are ruled willingly or by force (276c4–e14).[20] Thus, in just two pages they discuss how they made a mistake; they then discover they were mistaken about their first mistake; they also note that it is ambiguous as to how large the mistake was and whether it necessitated the whole myth, so that the myth itself may have been a mistake; they then proceed to make one distinction to resolve the dispute over the title of tender of the human herd, a distinction at odds with their earlier account of this dispute; and they subsequently discover a second mistake, which forced another distinction, even though they appeared to have finished their search. Despite all these hiccups, backtracks, false starts, and false stops, Young Socrates still proudly proclaims, "It does risk being the case, Stranger, that the demonstration (ἀπόδειξις) concerning the statesman would in this way be perfectly complete (τελέως)" (277a1–2).

---

[20] The Stranger says this distinction holds of human caretaking (τὴν ἀνθρωπίνην ἐπιμελητικὴν), that is, the caretaking either of or by human beings: we are not free to choose our god; we are, however, free to disobey him, and that alone may complicate god's rule (see Exodos 20:2–4, Judges 6:7–12, 8:22, 10:6–16, 21:25).

Whatever lessons Young Socrates may have learned from the myth, the human condition as one of essential resourcelessness in a cosmos not conducive to the precision of demonstration is not among them.

Young Socrates' assertion echoes the Stranger's earlier expectation that the myth would be sufficient for the demonstration or showing-forth (ἀπόδειξις) of the statesman (273e5–6; see 269c1–3). But as the Stranger now puts it, "they held (νομίσαντες) it fitting to make (ποιεῖσθαι) great models (μεγάλα παραδείγματα) for the king" (277b3–4). Drawing our attention to their shared root in the verb "to show" (δεικνύναι), the Stranger places two modes of showing alongside one another: demonstration or showing-forth (ἀπόδειξις), which proves its claims with the deductive clarity of mathematics, and generating images on the basis of a model, that is, something shown-alongside (παράδειγμα), which model's particularity always risks obscuring the matter under consideration, even as it elucidates it.[21] But strikingly, the Stranger suggests that the latter are implicit in the former (see Chapter IV, Section I on the *Apology of Socrates*). That said, even prior to the myth, we recall, the divisions relied on speculation about cranes and hearsay about the fish of the Nile (263d3–4, 264b12–c5). Indeed, the present passage might even serve as a long-delayed justification of his use of the model (παράδειγμα) of the angler and the metaphor of rivers and meadows at the outset of the *Sophist*. Accordingly, the *Statesman*'s second methodological digression, on the necessity of models to demonstration, continues the trilogy's examination of the relationship between the logical and the analogical, between being and the beautiful.[22] The Stranger emphasizes this relationship by comparing their method to poor sculpting or the sketching of an outline prior

---

[21] On the Stranger's juxtaposition of ἀπόδειξις and παράδειγμα, see Klein 1977, 163–66.

[22] The recurrence of ontology and the problem of images in all three dialogues suffices to show why Benardete gave his largest work on the trilogy the initially counterintuitive title, *The Being of the Beautiful*. See Burger 2002, 139–44

to painting (277a3–c4). "It's difficult," the Stranger remarks, "without using models (παραδείγμασι) to display (ἐνδείκνυσθαί) anything of the greater things. For each of us runs the risk of knowing everything as if in a dream and then again is ignorant of everything as it is in waking" (277d1–4).[23] In its emphasis on wakeful ignorance as following a dream of knowing, the Stranger's remark implies the Socratic observation that all who claim to know not only don't know but also don't know that they don't know, while those who know only know that they don't know (*Sophist* 231b3–8, *Apology of Socrates* 23a7–b4). Still more, in its emphasis on dreaming, in particular, it suggests the necessity of beginning from the beautiful (or, rather, noble) when posing the question of the good life. The Stranger, then, does not put Young Socrates through the methodological ringer merely in order to stifle the youth's pride in precision; rather, he does it so as to bring him closer to his elder namesake's understanding of what philosophy is (*Sophist* 216c2–d2).

Because Young Socrates struggles to understand "the experience (πάθος) in us concerning knowledge" (277d7), the Stranger next elaborates upon models. For this, he uses a model. The Stranger thus places Young Socrates, ever eager for clarity, at two removes from his goal: he will get a model for models before getting the model for statecraft, only after which they can apply the latter model and, he hopes, thereby find the statesman. The preliminary model the Stranger uses is one familiar from the *Sophist* and *Theaetetus*: letters.[24] Appealing again to Theaetetus' and Young Socrates' experiences, the Stranger explains that children who perceive adequately (ἱκανῶς διαισθάνονται; see *Sophist* 253d7) the elements in the shortest and easiest syllables can be deceived in opinion and speech in different syllables (277e2–278a4; see *Theaetetus* 207d8–e6). The best correction for such errors is to set the things,

---

[23] The return of the metaphor of dreaming recalls Socrates' dream at the end of the *Theaetetus*, in which Socratic philosophy once again and for the last time collapsed with the sophistry of Protagoras (see Act Two, Scene Two).

[24] Helpful for connecting these passages is Miller 2016.

about which they opine correctly, alongside (παρατιθέμενα) those they don't know, so as to allow for the showing (δειχθῇ) of which elements are truly opined (278a5–c7).[25] The Stranger then asks Young Socrates whether they would wonder if their soul had experienced (πεπονθυία) this same thing with regard to the elements of all things (278c8–d6). The hope is that, like words, the things of concern to us (πραγμάτων) will be compounds or syllables (συλλαβάς) made up of simple, discrete elements or letters (στοιχεῖα). Socrates and Theaetetus had proposed and rejected just this ontological hope the day before (*Theaetetus* 205e6–206a9). Additionally, it appears to be the necessary precondition to the acquisition of the dialectical science (*Sophist* 252e9–253c3). Accordingly, the Stranger expresses it as an hypothesis (278e4: ταῦτα εἰ ταύτῃ πέφυκεν). Young Socrates, however, says that he would find nothing wondrous should this be the case (278d7). For ease of reference, let us call the image constructed off this model *the ontology of method*, that is, how being must be for method to be possible—for thinking through images constructed on the basis of models (παραδείγματα) not to undermine but rather to aid in the acquisition of knowledge. Only thus will the latency of models in a demonstration not restrict our knowledge to knowledge of ignorance but allow for wakefulness in its entirety (278e4–11).

Because the Stranger will now use a model to exhibit the look (ἰδέα) of statecraft, and that model will occupy them until the end of the conversation, the remainder of the *Statesman* can be understood as an implicit test of the ontology of method. It cannot be stressed enough, however, that the goal of showing statecraft's look, such that all other arts possess a distinct form or species (εἶδος),

---

[25] The Stranger's exposition relies on an analysis of the word παράδειγμα into its constituents παρά and δείκνυμι: τιθέναι παρά (278a9): παραβάλλοντας (b1): παρατιθέμενα (4): παραθέμενος (279a8); ἐνδεικνύναι (278b1): δειχθῇ, δειχθέντα (4). He thus approaches the phenomenal basis to the methodic.

means that no other art can serve as a wholly adequate model. Rather, statecraft's distinctive features will emerge only upon the eventual breakdown of the model. In other words, the remainder of the dialogue serves as a *modus tollens* on the possibility of a mathematically precise alternative to Socratic political philosophy. It is in this breakdown that the Stranger hopes to show Young Socrates the Socratic observation of our dreamlike knowledge and wakeful ignorance, along with its connection to the beautiful or noble as the point of entry to the question of the connection between the good and the true (see Chapter IV, Section IV). That the Stranger does indeed harbor this hope is immediately clear upon a comparison of the exposition of the model with its application to statecraft. As his model, the Stranger selects weaving—more specifically, the weaving of cloaks (279a7–b6). His reason for this choice initially seems to be that, just as statecraft must, per the myth, serve the purpose of not experiencing the experience or occurrence (πάθος) of man's essential resourcelessness, so too the weaving of cloaks serves the purpose of not experiencing—or, better, of not being affected by—something ([ἕνεκα] τοῦ μὴ πάσχειν) (279c7–9).[26] Additionally, the discussion of weaving proceeds in three stages: an initial separation from the other arts (279b8–280a7), a more detailed repetition of that separation for the purposes of clarification (280a8–281c1), and finally the final separation from the closer but subordinate arts that help bring the weave into being (281c2–283a9). Likewise, the discussion of statecraft began with an initial separation of statecraft from the other arts, and soon there will be a second, more detailed account of that separation (287b4–303d3). And they will finally separate statecraft from the closely related arts of generalship, the judicial art, and rhetoric (303d4–305e7). They conclude thereafter by specifying what and how the statesman weaves, thus bringing together model and image (305e8–311c10). There will, however, be an important deviation from the model, as the Stranger takes a digression during the second stage, the more detailed account of the

---

[26] Cropsey also draws this connection (Cropsey 1995, 122).

initial separation.[27] This digression will elaborate upon the distinctive difference between weaving and statecraft, that is, the point at which the model of weaving proves inadequate as a guide to understanding the statesman: the necessity of inviolable law and the obstacle it poses to scientific statecraft (291a1–303d3). It is here, therefore, that we will catch a glimpse of what gives statecraft a look distinct from all other arts and sciences.

If it is only by deviating from the method that we come to see what makes statecraft unique, then Young Socrates' curiosity could never be reconciled with his love of precision and consequent attraction to methodology. He must make a choice. To set up this dilemma, the Stranger first elaborates upon the activity of the weaver. Now, in the *Cratylus*, Socrates says that the weaver's tool is the pinbeater or comb (κερκίς) (*Cratylus* 388c5–6). According to the Stranger in the *Sophist*, its use belongs under the class of arts that divide or discriminate (διακριτική) (*Sophist* 226b1–c9). Aristotle supports the Stranger's initial classification, noting that the use of the comb is restricted to separation (δίωσις) (Aristotle, *Physics* VII.2.243b6–7). Precisely what sort of separation it accomplishes is clear again from the *Cratylus*, where Socrates says that one uses the comb to divide (διακρίνομεν) the entangled warp and woof (*Cratylus* 388b1–3). In the *Statesman*, however, the comb is said to serve two purposes, half of its use belonging under diacritics (διακριτική)—the class of arts that divide—with the other half belonging under syncritics (συγκριτική)—the class of arts that com-

---

[27] A more precise account of the structure of the *Statesman* would have to take into account two other deviations. First, the search for the statesman requires a παράδειγμα, while the model of the weaver (like the angler) required none. Second, and perhaps similarly, whereas the weaver had to be separated first from the cognate (συγγενεῖς) arts and then the co-causal (συναιτίαι) arts, the statesman is separated first from the co-causal arts and then the cognate arts. For the relevant instances of συγγενεῖς see 280b3, 5, 298b1, 303d5, e1, 303e9–10, 306c5 and of συναιτίαι see 281c4, d11, e4, 9, 287b7, c9, d3, 289c9.

bine (282b1–c4). And, still more, the Stranger concludes his discussion of weaving by classifying it as the proper part of the syncritics that's in wool-working (τὸ…συγκριτικῆς τῆς ἐν ταλασιουργίᾳ μόριον) (282c5–283a9). According to the Stranger, then, the comb appears to be primarily a syncritical tool, in that it puts together what belongs together but are apart, with a subordinate and corrective diacritical role, in that it divides what is together but belong apart. That is, the syncritical role supplies the end at which weaving aims, with the diacritical disentanglement of warp and woof being an occasional, and thus not always necessary, means toward that end.[28] It is on precisely this point, we will see, that the model breaks down: the diacritical component of the statesman's art will prove essential to his task—indeed, it will be the very core of it.

To prepare Young Socrates for the eventual breakdown of the model of weaving, the Stranger goes on the dialogue's third and final methodological digression. Fearing that his exposition of the model of weaving has been too lengthy, the Stranger pauses before applying it to statecraft; he reflects, specifically, on how they have been talking in circles (ἐν κύκλῳ) and thus on the difficulty of speaking at the appropriate length (283b1–3). Young Socrates of course says nothing was in vain, glutton that he is (283b4–5). The Stranger is inclined to agree but notes that someone might nevertheless opine otherwise (283b6–c1). Stepping away from their task, the Stranger remarks that, when praising or blaming the length of a speech, one must do so not simply for its being longer or shorter than most speeches—not simply according to relative measure (πρὸς

---

[28] The Stranger's treatment of combing appears to be a complex joke. In the *Sophist*, the Stranger put combing entirely under διακριτική (*Sophist* 226b2–c9). Here, in the *Statesman*, one half of combing belongs under διακριτική, the other under συγκριτική (282b1–c4). By the end of the *Statesman*, however, statecraft's version of combing will be understood wholly under συγκριτική (310e5–311a2). The Stranger separates and combines the elements of combing, playfully inviting or, rather, compelling us to consider how his description of statecraft relates to his own activity of pairing and parting and thus to the pairing and parting of the philosopher, as well.

ἄλληλα)—but for being longer or shorter than is fitting—for missing the measure of the mean or due measure (πρὸς τὸ μέτριον) (283c3–e13). The latter measure not only applies to their discussion but is additionally necessary to the arts and their works, weaving and statecraft included; for only with reference to such a measure as supplies a standard of fittingness can we praise what these arts produce as good and beautiful (284a1–b6). Though necessary to the arts and, indeed, promising to supply the connection between the good and the true, still the measure of the mean (τὸ μέτριον) appears to be elusive, if it even is at all.[29] For one, the Stranger says that they must *compel* (προσαναγκαστέον) more and less to become measurable with respect to "the becoming of the measure of the mean" (284b7–c6).[30] The Stranger also remarks that they will eventually need "a demonstration concerning the precise itself" (τὴν περὶ αὐτὸ τἀκριβὲς ἀπόδειξιν), treating its existence as necessary to the perfection of the arts but as nevertheless hypothetical (284c7–d9, esp. d7–9). If not demonstrated, then, the precise itself is—for us, at least—an image of uncertain veracity, a result that cannot help but be dissatisfying. In short, immediately after presenting a model for statecraft, the Stranger raises a methodological question that casts doubt on our ability to know whether or not mathematical precision has been attained or could ever be attained, be it for statecraft or for speeches.

By what criterion, then, are we to praise or blame the length of a speech, if not by being the precisely fitting speech, the speech of due measure? The Stranger presents an alternative standard by which to judge the length of a speech, and this finally brings us to his second articulation of the aim of their conversation, namely, that they put forward the search for the statesman not for its own sake

---

[29] Hence Aristotle characterizes moral virtue as skilled in *aiming* at the mean (στοχαστικὴ τοῦ μέσου) (*Nicomachean Ethics* II.9.1109a20–24). I owe this observation to Michael Davis.

[30] Indeed, he compares this compulsion to the compulsion they felt in the *Sophist* to make non-being be, and the results of that compulsion were, we discovered, uncompelling.

but for the sake of becoming more dialectical (285d5–7). Accordingly, in response to the person blaming the length of their speeches, the argument advises them not to be concerned with the speed and ease of the search as much as "to honor most of all and firstly the pursuit or method (τὴν μέθοδον) of being capable (δυνατὸν) of dividing according to forms (εἴδη)" (286d6–e1), that is, the acquisition of—or gradual approximation of one's search to—the dialectical science. Consequently, the purpose of any speech is to make him listening more capable of discovery (εὑρετικώτερον), more "heuretical" (286e1–4). And for that, one must allow the way or method to take such byways or circuitous excursions (τὰς ἐν κύκλῳ περιόδους) as it did with weaving (283b3: ἐν κύκλῳ), that is, to venture off even when there's every risk that one will return with little to show for one's efforts in terms of the immediate goal; for, though such excursions lengthen the speech and make the overall path to the immediate goal more difficult, still they may achieve— perhaps even by virtue of their very failure to produce more results— the larger and more primary goal of making one's associates more dialectical and more capable of discovering a means of clarifying (δηλώσεως) the beings in speech (286e4–287a6). This less precise understanding of the praise and blame of a speech has the merit of incorporating the lesson of the *Sophist* on the dialectical science, namely, that we are never in possession of, but rather are always on the way to, such a science. More fundamentally, however, the Stranger points to a way of understanding the good in truth as the necessary but elusive object of inquiry (see Chapter IV, Section IV, third to last paragraph).

That will have to wait, of course, for our return to the *Theaetetus* in Chapter Four. As for the *Statesman*, the Stranger, by appealing to Young Socrates' love of method and presenting method as in part unmethodical, creates an incentive for the youth to give his curiosity priority over his love of precision. The test for whether the Stranger's warning to Young Socrates has been successful will turn on whether the youth will be willing to deviate from the model of weaving. The Stranger suggests as much by employing the word byway, period, or excursion (περίοδος) outside the myth and, more specifically, during a discussion of methodology. If the human condition is characterized by essential resourcelessness and perplexity, then the ontology of method cannot hold. But Young Socrates will notice this only through the breakdown of the model of weaving, the consequent deviation from their method or path (μέθοδος) onto a by-way or excursion (περίοδος), and the resulting discovery of epistemic heterogeneity—that is, the distinct look of statecraft that shows all other arts are of a single species. It is in anticipation of this eventuality that the Stranger now turns to apply the model of the weaver to the statesman (287a6–b3).

III.

The series of methodological digressions over the course of the *Statesman* have incorporated into its argument many of the lessons of the *Sophist*, not least the problem of acquiring the dialectical science, the very problem that made it impossible to distinguish with certainty the sophist from the philosopher. With the last of these digressions completed, it comes as no surprise that the dialogue's argument becomes much easier to follow, as the conversation's trajectory proceeds linearly following the model of the weaver, that is, without revision or backtracking. Whereas the Stranger had deliberately delayed communicating the point of the myth until it was over, he will henceforth follow the plan pre-determined by their model. Nevertheless, the apparent clarity of the argument's path should not fool us, as the Stranger has warned Young Socrates to be prepared to wander off course, to interrupt the path (μέθοδος) with an excursion (περίοδος). The dialogue's increased clarity may reflect less the subject matter than Young Socrates' tendency to accept solutions too readily out of a pride in the capabilities of human reason and a concomitant eagerness to define the scientific statesman once and for all. There is every danger, then, that his pride and eagerness will blind him to what's distinctive about statecraft. Is it the virtues of their model or rather the vices of Young Socrates that lead the conversation to proceed so smoothly?

Though the conversation proceeds more smoothly, the application of the model of weaving does not produce a simple one-to-one correspondence. We recall that the discussion of weaving proceeded in three stages: the initial separation (279b8–280a7), the more detailed repetition (280a8–281c1), and the final separation from the closer but subordinate arts that help bring the weave into being (281c2–283a9). The first half or so of the *Statesman* discussed in Section II corresponds to the first part of the discussion of weaving, that is, the initial separation from the other arts. As he returns from the last methodological digression, the Stranger immediately takes up the task of separating statecraft from all the other arts once again (287b4–d6), turning only much later to the more closely related yet subordinate arts (303d4–e5). Despite this apparent one-to-one correspondence, the second and central stage of repeating the separating of statecraft from the rest of the arts contains a digression on law that elucidates what makes statecraft distinctive from all other arts. Despite its imperfections, the Stranger will argue, law is necessary to statecraft, for without it the statesman cannot hope to give guidance to all citizens at once; but because law lays claim to an inviolability uncharacteristic of the writings of other arts, it restricts the statesman's ability to correct for its necessary imperfections. By taking this excursion (περίοδος) on law, then, the Stranger indicates to Young Socrates the phenomenon that gives statecraft its distinctive look (ἰδέα): inviolable law. What's more, this distinctive feature to statecraft will, it turns out, stand as an invitation to charlatans and imitators—to the sophist. Thus, it is here that we will finally come to see the sophist's primary apparition (φάντασμα), that of the statesman; we surmise, too, that we will also come to learn of the place of the philosopher in relation to his twin apparitions. Consequently, nothing less hangs in the balance, in their application of the model of weaving to statecraft, than the whole purpose of the trilogy: Plato's defense of Socrates, of the problem of Socrates, before the tribunal of science.

The sophist's return is at first surprising. The Stranger begins by going through seven kinds (γένη) of arts, the fifth of which—the imitative arts or arts producing playthings—presumably includes sophistics (287d1–289a6, esp. 288c1–d1; see *Sophist* 234a7). Before turning to the eighth kind—that of slaves and servants, in which he locates the statesman—the Stranger recapitulates the preceding in a list, with the imitative arts now in the sixth place, its "just" location (289a7–c3). The Stranger then divides the eighth kind into three further kinds—slaves proper, those involved in exchange, and heralds and priests—thus producing ten kinds overall (289c4–290e9). It is here that the Stranger comes across the eleventh, which contains "some quite strange ones," "a certain kind of every tribe" (πάμφυλόν τι γένος), "resembling lions and centaurs and others of this sort, and very many satyrs and the wily beasts without strength" (291a1–c2). Initially just a part of the city, the imitative kind proliferates itself across the city as a whole. This unexpected proliferation is reflected in the imitative's shifting place from the fifth of seven to the sixth, so that when the group grows to eleven it becomes central—fittingly, too, as the eleventh includes, finally, "the greatest sorcerer or charlatan (γόητα) of all the sophists and most experienced in this art" (291c3–4). That is, by suddenly disrupting the inquiry into statecraft, the imitative makes itself central to the city as such. Whereas in the *Sophist* the sophist portrayed himself as competent in all things, in the *Statesman* he assumes his place at the helm of the city, in the place of the statesman. We thus finally find ourselves before the sophist's primary apparition, latent in but missing from the argument of the *Sophist*. Consequently, our question going into the digression is, first, how the sophist imitates the statesman in particular and, second, what light this might shed on his imitation of the philosopher, as well.

It is not immediately clear precisely who this greatest sorcerer or charlatan of all sophists is. In his elaboration, the Stranger provides a regime analysis, first distinguishing them numerically: a regime may be ruled by one man, a few men, or the multitude (291c9–d9). He then distinguishes between better and worse forms of each regime—save democracy, rule by the multitude—in accordance with a number of factors but primarily, it turns out, in accordance with whether the rule is lawful or lawless (ἀνομίαν) (291d10–292a4; see 302c8–303b7). This alone, it appears to Young Socrates, suffices to determine which regime is correct (292a5–10). The Stranger, however, points out that the boundary (ὅρον) separating the statesman from all others had nothing to do with the number of rulers or whether the rule was forcible or voluntary, but rather with whether it was a certain science (292b1–d10). And, because so venerable a science is not liable to being possessed by many men—let alone very many—but only by "some one, two, and altogether few," most of these regimes are, despite having just appeared to be "correct," in fact flawed (292e1–293a5; see *Meno* 90b4–92e6, *Apology of Socrates* 24d7–25a11). Thus, regardless of the manner of the rule—whether in accordance with laws or without laws (ἐάντε κατὰ νόμους ἐάντε ἄνευ νόμων)—so long as it is by science that this ruler rules, then his rule is correct (293a6–d2). Young Socrates responds that the Stranger's articulation is beautiful, even as the Stranger compares the statesman to a doctor who must on occasion use surgery and cautery outside of what medical writings prescribe (293d3). He does not consider how the image of cutting and burning, when translated from medicine into politics, entails killing, exiling, colonization, and the naturalization of large numbers of immigrants (293d4–e6). Only after the Stranger has translated these features of medicine into politics does Young Socrates express concern about the claim that the scientific statesman rules without laws (293e7–9). Contrary to what Theodorus surmised, the measure of the mean (τὸ μέτριον) does not preclude harshness (see *Sophist* 216b7–c1). That Young Socrates does not on his own explore the implications of the Stranger's temporary model only adds to our suspicion that he is not attending to the method sufficiently. That said, as regards our question concerning the identity of the greatest sorcerer or charlatan of all sophists, we suspect that the Stranger places in that group all regimes and rulers, save the scientific statesman.

To understand what that might mean, we must follow the Stranger on his excursion (περίοδος) on law, during which he articulates the twofold activity of the statesman's art in a manner that recalls the twofold activity of the weaver's comb (κερκίς). The Stranger says that, though the legislative art does belong in some manner to that of the statesman, the best thing is not for laws but for the kingly man with prudence or intelligence (φρόνησις) to hold sway or to have strength or power (ἰσχύειν) (294a6–8). Because of the dissimilarities among human beings and actions and, in addition, because they are never in any way at rest or at peace (ἡσυχίαν), a law would never be capable of comprehending the best and the most just for all precisely (ἀκριβῶς) (294a10–b7).[31] At the same time, the foolish striving of law to enjoin the best makes it recalcitrant to any deviation from it, even should the statesman discover something new that appears better (294b8–c9). Nevertheless, legislation remains necessary, inasmuch as one man could never be sufficient (ἱκανός) to sit beside each and every person and assign what is fitting for each individual (294c10–295b6). But for the very same reason that legislation may be necessary, such lawlessness or deviations from the law (ἀνομία) as shocked Young Socrates may too, on occasion, be necessary; in such circumstances, the statesman will have to dare (τολμῶντα) to violate the ancestral things (τἀρχαῖα) (295b7–296a4). Like the art of the weaver, then, the statesman's art has both a syncritical component and a corrective, diacritical component: the construction and the dissolution of laws. Outside the digression on law, the Stranger refers to the statesman as a legislator only three times: twice in the context of the relationship between statesman and judge, as is to be expected (305b5, c2), and once in the context of the statesman's weaving together of the moderate and manly souls in the city (309d1). The opinions that form what the

---

[31] It should be noted that the Stranger merely assumes a fluxist doctrine. This has to do, I think, with the rejection of divine providence in the myth.

Stranger calls the "divine bond" are nothing but the laws, be they written or unwritten.[32]

One senses here that the Stranger is combining two earlier elements from the dialogue: the cosmology and the third methodological digression. According to the cosmology, corporeal things have an innate tendency to collapse into "a limitless sea of dissimilarity" (273d6–e1), a tendency most pronounced in our age, the so-called age of Zeus. Thus, what necessitates a change in the law is when things come to be otherwise than the usual things—what the Stranger refers to as the things from Zeus that are contrary to one's hope or expectation (παρὰ τὴν ἐλπίδα) (295d1–2). In response, man turns to the arts as a way out of his state of having no recourse or resource, of being trapped in a cosmos rife with great perplexities (μεγάλαι ἀπορίαι). When we confronted this image of the human condition earlier, we asked how statecraft could actually provide against such essential resourcelessness. The third methodological digression in turn argued that the arts could not be without the existence of and the artisans' access to the precise itself. At that point, we were dissatisfied with the Stranger's avoidance of the question whether the precise itself is accessible or even exists. Now, however, we see the reason for his avoidance: by having assumed the best case

---

[32] It is difficult at first to make out how the Stranger views the relationship between writing, law, and statecraft. Occasionally, he speaks as though law and writing are one and the same, as when he uses the phrase καὶ μετὰ γραμμάτων καὶ ἄνευ νόμων (292a8; compare 293a7, b3–4, 295a7, b2–5, b10–c5, 300b1–6, c1–2). In accordance with this, he also opposes the writings to art (297a1–2, 299b3–6, e4–5). At other times, however, he indicates that one can legislate without laws, as with γράψαντι καὶ ἄγραφα νομοθετήσαντι (295e5; see, also, 299c3–4). He appears to have in mind the ancestral things, that is, τὰ παλαιά, τὰ πάτρια, or even τὰ ἔθη (296c9–10, 298d7–e1, 299a3–4, 301a3–4, e9). Hence he at one point uses the phrase ἄγραφα πάτρια (298e1). There are, then, written and unwritten laws, the latter of which are the ancestral practices or habits and both of which are contrary to the statesman's art. And though the statesman could well legislate either form of law, it is primarily through written law that he ensures the persistence of his legislation.

scenario—that it exists and that we have access to it—the Stranger is able to bring out why the statesman must issue laws, that is, why necessity dictates a necessarily imprecise means. Even if the statesman could discern the good in truth, the best thing to do in each and every situation, the practical necessity of laws requires that we deviate from the true—that in legislation we act unscientifically. Accordingly, the properly scientific part of statecraft is not the act of legislation, which belongs to statecraft only in a certain manner (τρόπον...τινά) (294a6–7), but rather begins from or is wholly constituted by the diacritical examination of the scientific deficiency of the law. This constitutes a marked departure from the model of weaving. For weaving, the diacritical disentanglement of warp and woof was subordinate to the syncritical component of completing the weave, so that the syncritical provided the end and the diacritical the merely circumstantial or accidental means to attaining that end. For statecraft, however, the situation is quite the reverse. Because the syncritical component is necessarily flawed, it is subordinate to the diacritical component, that is, the exposure of the scientific inadequacy of the laws in light of the standard—however elusive—of the precise itself. The law, the Stranger remarks, derives its strength or force (ῥώμη) from the statesman's art and, indeed, his soul (296e4–297a5 with 259c8); it is in the light of science that the laws are to be judged.

Statecraft, therefore, would appear to be unique among the arts in that it *must* act imprecisely if it is to act at all—the statesman's weave, as it were, cannot protect against all contingencies and so of necessity allows some unforeseeable harm (see 279c7–9). Whereas the trainer may, as he pleases, teach either individuals or groups, and so act with precision or imprecisely, the statesman has no choice. Even in the age of Kronos, the Stranger remarked, the god made use of divine helpers (271d3–8, 272e6–7). The Stranger thus indicates that it is law that gives statecraft, as he said, a unique look and so groups the other arts and sciences into a single species. Of course, we are still in the dark as to what the diacritical core of statecraft is. We suspect, of course, that this activity, as a critical unraveling of the limited veracity of the opinions that law or custom has embedded in our souls, has a deep kinship with Socratic political philosophy. And we suspect, further, that this relationship will become all the more clear once the Stranger has disentangled the statesman from "the greatest sorcerer or charlatan of all the sophists." Toward that end, the Stranger imagines what might occur when the statesman returns from some time away and seeks to enact things contrary to what has been set down as law (295b10–c5). In such situations, the many hold that the statesman must persuade them (296a5–11). Should such persuasion fail, however, force may be necessary (296b1–4). But then the statesman's compulsion would appear to the many to be ugly, unjust, and bad (296b5–d6). One senses here the Stranger's definition of an apparition (φάντασμα) in the *Sophist*, namely, as "what appears to resemble the beautiful (τὸ φαινόμενον...ἐοικέναι τῷ καλῷ) because the viewing [is] not from [a] beautiful [position or person] (οὐκ ἐκ καλοῦ)" (*Sophist* 236b4–5). Would law, therefore, be an apparition and law-abidingness an essentially defective, even ugly thing? The Stranger suggests as much by saying that all regimes not governed by the scientific statesman imitate (μιμουμένας) his rule, some more beautifully and others more shamefully or in an uglier manner (297b7–c4). The Stranger's use of the comparative confirms our suspicion that, because the statesman must dilute his art through legislation, *all* regimes would possess some ugliness. Only the scientific statesman's rule could be beautiful—or, rather, noble. One suspects, therefore, that the lions, centaurs, and satyrs of which the Stranger spoke are the multifarious, apparently limitless customs and regimes to be found from time to time and place to place. Enchanting though they may be, still by the light of science they are but ugly monstrosities, fictitious non-entities.

Thankfully, Young Socrates asks the Stranger to clarify what he means when he calls these regimes imitations (μιμημάτων) (297c5–6). The Stranger's elaboration takes two stages. In the first, he shows how the multitude imitate the syncritical component of statecraft, namely, legislation. Returning to the image of the physician and ship-captain, the Stranger paints a picture of the many rebelling against such artisans—for example, when an accident happens on the ocean or a medical treatment proves unbearably painful; instead of consulting these experts, the many deliberate on what should be done and set down their resolutions as the law governing medical and navigational practices (297e8–298e3). Young Socrates rightly remarks that such behavior would be altogether strange (ἄτοπα) (298e4). Continuing, the Stranger notes that under such circumstances, where none is held to be wiser than the laws, whoever so much as *searches* for an art of medicine or piloting would appear the garrulous sophist, guilty of corrupting the youth (299b3–d1).[33] Asked by the Stranger how things would look under such practices, Young Socrates responds that, with even the search forbidden, the arts would perish and the current difficulty of life would become so great as to be in every way unlivable (299d1–e10). Though he disparages law established by popular fiat, the Stranger clarifies in the second stage of the argument that the still greater evil would be the entire disregard for such laws as are made by the artisan; for, if deviations from the law are too easily tolerated—that is,

---

[33] As many have noted (see, for example, Howland 1998, 323 n. 71), the Stranger's language here recalls that of Socrates' indictment; this in turn raises a number of interesting questions that are, unfortunately, too speculative to answer. Is this only Plato's allusion, or is it the Stranger's, too? If the latter, has the Stranger already learned of Socrates' indictment, even before meeting him? That is, did Theodorus ask, after our version of the *Theaetetus* ends, what indictment Socrates went to receive and then report that to the Stranger prior to the beginning of the *Sophist*? Did Socrates even know then the content of the indictment? Does that show that, despite his ostensible remove from political affairs, Theodorus found some vindication in learning of Socrates' new legal troubles? And might the Stranger be there not simply to punish Socrates, as Socrates fears, but out of an interest in this peculiar criminal? However we answer these questions, whether we can even answer them, the importance of this passage cannot be overstated: the language suggests that it is central to the trilogy, while also situating the trilogy with in the larger context of Socrates' two trials.

if room is made for the popular persuasion of which the Stranger earlier spoke—then the result will be such deviations as are guided by profit and private enjoyment (χάριτος ἰδίας), rather than those guided by art and much experience (πείρας) (300a1–b7). Such is especially the case with the tyrant, who makes himself out (προσποιῆται) to be the knowing ruler by acting neither in accordance with laws nor in accordance with custom (ἔθη) (301b10–c4). The statesman thus finds himself caught between two charlatans: on one side, the many usurp power from the statesman by coopting for themselves his legislative function; on the other side, the tyrant supplies an imitation (μιμήματος) of the sort of argument the statesman might give the people in order to justify to them his deviation from the ancestral laws. The one imitates the syncritical component of statecraft, the other the diacritical.

The statesman thus finds himself in the following predicament. Given that he can practice his art only imprecisely by means of law, the statesman opens himself up to criticism from the many when these laws necessarily fail to provide what is best in all circumstances. This usurpation on the part of the many in turn forbids as unwise any deviation from what is legislated by popular approval. But should the statesman actually succeed in persuading the many to deviate from his or their laws, he necessarily opens the door to those who imitate his rationale, the chief such imitator being the tyrant. Forced to give laws as imitations of his prudence or wisdom, the statesman opens himself up to being imitated in turn. It is in this that the uniqueness of the statesman's art consists.[34] Contrary to our earlier suspicion, then, Young Socrates appears to notice the statesman's peculiarity. For when the Stranger constructs a semblance (εἰκόνας, ἀπεικάζειν) of the other arts on the basis of statecraft, Young Socrates finds the result utterly strange. That is, he detects, however faintly, that the look (ἰδέα) of statecraft is unique. Of

---

[34] For a treatment of the relationship between prudence (φρόνησις) and law (νόμος) in the *Statesman*, in light of the distinction between εἰκαστική and φανταστική in the *Sophist*, see Speliotis 2011.

course, we worry that he takes this uniqueness as indication that politics needs to undergo a scientific revolution; he does, after all, lament quite powerfully that, should the use of law extend to other arts and sciences, it would be the cause of much ill (299e6–10). Perhaps for this reason the Stranger is careful to emphasize that, given the above predicament, the scientific statesman includes among his legislation the prohibition of all deviation from the laws; this, the Stranger says, is the statesman's second sailing, that is, a second best option once the first proves impossible—the truly best option, as opposed to the imagined best (300c1–3). As for Young Socrates, whether he has taken to heart the Stranger's emphasis on the necessary imprecision of statecraft turns on the question of whether he will call for the proper excursion (περίοδος) from their path (μέθοδος), namely, an investigation into the diacritical core of statecraft.

Having finally separated the statesman from his imposters—from the greatest imitators and charlatans or sorcerers (μιμητὰς καὶ γόητας) occupying the ranks of the various regimes—the Stranger turns in the final stage of the argument to distinguish the statesman from those with kindred yet subordinate arts, namely, the general, the judge, and the rhetorician (303b8–304a5).[35] Each in its own way is subservient to the statesman yet has the potential to usurp his place: the rhetorician by exploiting his ability to persuade through

---

[35] Note that, of all the arts in the city, these three alone are granted the honor of being supra-sophistic arts: though the three are to statecraft like copper, silver, and unbreakable stuff (ἀδάμας) are to gold, the motley tribe is according to this analogy (κατὰ τὸν αὐτὸν...λόγον) but earth and stones (303c8–304a2). The higher honor appears to be due to their relationship not primarily to this or that regime, to these or those laws; that is, though persuasion, war, and adjudication may involve law, they nevertheless also encroach upon the just and unjust, enmity and friendship, and the like (see 303e10–304a2, 304e9–11, 305b4–c5). Indeed, inasmuch as persuasion proceeds through μυθολογία, the rhetorician could himself (or in conjunction with the statesman) usurp the place of the prophet or herald (304c10–d3 with 260d11–261a1).

mythology (μυθολογίας) (304a6–e2; see *Gorgias* 456b6–c7, 523a1–2), the general by inferring from his knowledge of how to win a war that he knows too whether it is better to wage war or make peace (304e3–305a10; see *Laches* 198e2–199a3), and the judge by entertaining bribes or allowing pity to sway his judgments (305b1–c9; see *Apology of Socrates* 34b7–c7). The Stranger concludes that the statesman does not himself act but rules those capable of acting; that is, the cognitive status of the art puts it at the beginning of action with respect to the opportune and inopportune (ἐγκαιρίας τε πέρι καὶ ἀκαιρίας), while the others merely do those things that the statesman has enjoined (305c10–d6). The language here recalls again the third methodological digression, which presented the arts as measuring relative to, among other things, the opportune (τὸν καίρον) (284e7). But the matter is complicated by the fact that, as the Stranger now says, statecraft rules not only these three arts but the laws, as well (305d7–e7). That is, the statesman deems it opportune to tend after what necessarily miss the opportune. The digression on law thus intrudes upon the later discussion and threatens to break down the model of weaving. It is now, if ever, that Young Socrates should be poised to object to a neat application of the model of weaving, so much has the Stranger prepared him.

The Stranger finally turns to the statesman as a sort of weaver, namely, to how he weaves and what woven thing he produces (306a1–4). He begins by outlining a tension within virtue, a tension not acknowledged by the common opinion that the parts of virtue are friendly with one another (306a5–b13). The tension is evident, the Stranger elaborates, in our admiration (ἀγασθῶμεν, ἀγασθέντες) and praise of quickness and intensity of action as manliness or courage (ἀνδρείας) and of quietness and slowness of action as moderate (σωφρονικά), so long as these actions are done at the opportune time (ἐν καιρῷ) (306b13–307b4). But when they are inopportune (ἄκαιρα), we blame the quick and intense as hubristic and crazy and the quiet and slow as cowardly and lazy (307b5–c2). What the statesman must do, therefore, is exile the hubristic and enslave the lowly, so that only the best of each of the two contrary natures remain, namely, those receptive to the education the statesman prescribes (309a8–b7). These souls so distinguished, the statesman may then weave them together using what he calls a divine bond (θείῳ...δεσμῷ) (309c1–3). Pressed by Young Socrates to explain what he means (309b8, c4), the Stranger clarifies that he calls divine a true opinion that really is (ὄντως οὖσαν) about the beautiful, just, and good things, and the things contrary to these (309c5–9). Only the statesman and good legislator, the Stranger continues, is capable of implanting (ἐμποιεῖν) the divine bond in the souls of the citizen (309d1–5). The reference here to the law-giving part of the statesman's art gives one pause about whether the opinions instilled in these souls could ever be simply true, to say nothing of the failed attempts to distinguish true opinions from false in the *Theaetetus* and *Sophist*; we therefore wonder whether the manly soul will ever be sufficiently tamed and the orderly nature made sufficiently moderate and intelligent through the sort of general education that the laws provide (309d10–e9). The Stranger confirms our doubt when he claims, paradoxically, that these natures are nurtured and grow up in accordance with nature (κατὰ φύσιν) through laws (διὰ νόμων) (310a1–2). Far from being a solution, the phrase "in accordance with nature through laws" (κατὰ φύσιν διὰ νόμων) is rather a restatement of the problem. This means that the statesman's version of the weaver's syncritical use of the comb (κερκίς)—the combing-together (συγκερκίζοντα) of moderate and manly by means of common opinions (ὁμοδοξίαις), honors, dishonors, and the like—will *necessarily* miss the mark (310e7–311a2).

Though the Stranger coins the verb "to comb together" (συγκερκίζειν), he is silent about the correlative neologism "to comb apart" (διακερκίζειν). That is, as he wraps up their final definition, the Stranger discusses *only* the syncritical component of his art—namely, legislation—as the language of combination abounds (συμπλακὲν, ὁμονοίᾳ, φιλίᾳ, κοινὸν, συναγαγοῦσα, συνέχῃ); at the same time, however, the Stranger also ends with a qualification of the conclusion, adding that the scientific statesman accomplishes his goal "to the extent that it's suitable (προσήκει) for a city to come to be (γίγνεσθαι) happy" (311b7–c7). The return of the suitable in reference to becoming brings to mind the measure of the mean, that is, the measure according to the compulsory or necessary being of becoming (κατὰ τὴν τῆς γενέσεως ἀναγκαίαν οὐσίαν) (283d7–9). The issue, to which the Stranger's qualification points, concerns the extent to which the statesman is limited by the fittingness of happiness for a city, that is, by the ability of science or knowledge to attain the measure of the mean in politics—whether the statesman can achieve the good on the level of actual political practice or rather must dilute it through law. In effect, then, the Stranger ends with a qualification that, properly considered, should prompt Young Socrates to object that they had agreed that political science, the science of statecraft, necessarily acts with imprecision. The Stranger has given him ample reason to raise this objection and, indeed, the requisite resources to expand upon it. And should he have accepted the Stranger's invitation here, Young Socrates would necessarily have discovered that their examination of statecraft is by no means complete, as they have yet to expand upon its diacritical core. Young Socrates' response, however, is quite the contrary. "You have spoken very beautifully," he remarks. "Very beautifully, in turn, have you brought to completion (ἀπετέλεσας) for us, Stranger, the kingly and political man" (311c8–10). Young Socrates clearly has not learned his lesson (see 267c4–d2, 277a1–2). Whether or not the Stranger pointed out to Young Socrates his error we cannot say, for Plato ends his writing here. If we are to search for what is missing from the *Statesman*—and what is missing is essential—we must look elsewhere.

IV.

If the *Theaetetus* was the tragedy of the elder Socrates and the *Sophist* the tragedy of Theaetetus, then the *Statesman* completes the trilogy with the tragedy of Young Socrates. Though possessed of a digressive curiosity, Young Socrates never lets it get the better of his eagerness for a precise result. His willingness to wander only when it involves the pursuit of methodology forbids him access to the unmethodical side of thinking—the latency of models (παραδείγματα), and the images constructed thereupon, in any given demonstration (ἀπόδειξις), the inextricability of the analogical from the logical. In this way the Stranger completes his *modus tollens* on the ontology of method and therewith on a more scientific, Theodoran alternative to Socrates' appearance in the guises of sophist and statesman. Whereas the *Sophist* was the tragedy of Theaetetus' excessive humility, the *Statesman* is the tragedy of Young Socrates' excessive eagerness. The one fearfully fled from the sophist into mathematics, while the other willfully distorts politics through the application of mathematics to statecraft. Had Theaetetus been more courageous, he would have asked the Stranger what form the problem of spoken images takes in the sophist's primary apparition (φάντασμα) as the statesman, and thus found himself in the *Statesman*'s digression on law. And had Young Socrates been more moderate, he would have asked the Stranger to expand upon the diacritical core of statecraft, and thus found himself confronting the contradictor sophist, the examination of whom brought the *Sophist* to the dialectical science. As it stands, however, Theaetetus humbly sees himself as not as smart as Socrates and about as ugly (see *Theaetetus* 143e7–144a1, esp. ἧττον). Does the hubristic Young Socrates, then, think he's as smart as Socrates and much better looking, to boot—a Socrates made young and beautiful?

In contrast to the unmanly Theaetetus and the immoderate Young Socrates, the soul of Socrates appears to attain the proper mixing of moderation and courage, since, as Ronna would often point out, he moderately admits ignorance but courageously never gives up the quest for wisdom. If one could put together Theaetetus' looks with Young Socrates' name while mixing the souls of each in equal proportions, one would actually have made Socrates young and beautiful, or at least young and less ugly. Plato's Socrates is that mixture of moderation and courage, at which the statesman's legislation aims but of necessity misses. The Socratic model is also latent in the Stranger's own activity. In the *Sophist*, Theaetetus' hesitance before the proliferating perplexities forced the Stranger to offer positive results, that is, to provide. In the *Statesman*, however, he is pressed to point out, even invent mistakes, so as to slow down the impetuous Young Socrates. In the former, then, he dons the guise of the statesman-legislator, while in the latter he assumes the apparition of the sophist-contradictor. The Stranger in the *Statesman* is to the Stranger in the *Sophist* as the sophist is to the statesman, and as perplexity is to provision. The Stranger splits into Socrates' apparitions (φαντάσματα) even as he attempts to escape them, rendering himself—intentionally, I believe—no less elusive than his Athenian counterpart.[36] To understand him, then, is to understand what it means for a perplexity (ἀπορία) to be a provision (πόρος). In the *Theaetetus*, Socrates manages both to scare manly Young Socrates into silence and to encourage the timid Theaetetus into speaking (see *Theaetetus* 145e8–146a5, 148e1–6, 151d7–e1). As he sat in prison, repeating to Euclides time and again the conversation found in the *Theaetetus*, Socrates must have recognized that what he had accomplished there served as a response to the Stranger's Theodoran critique. By having Socrates document that conversation without its

---

[36] If, after the end of the *Statesman*, the Stranger corrected Young Socrates yet again, then this conclusion would be well founded. But if not, then it seems that the Stranger, in allowing Young Socrates to hold an inadequate but salutary opinion, has played the statesman. This conclusion is tempting for a number of reasons. First, it permits the following proportion: Protagoras : the Stranger : Socrates :: sophist : statesman : philosopher. Second, it shows that Theodorus' understanding of philosophy as science is, in its moralizing tendency and otherwise, closer to statecraft, and so no alternative to Socrates. Third and most importantly, like the statesman, the Stranger agrees in the *Sophist* to obey a divine law that the myth in the *Statesman* suggests he does not believe to be true, namely, Zeus' law of ξενία. Whereas Protagoras used his relativism to table the question of the gods (*Theaetetus* 162c2–7 with d4–e2), Socrates held that the γένη of philosopher and god are nearly equal in opacity (*Sophist* 216b8–c4). The Stranger appears to agree with Socrates, though he acts more in accordance with piety. On the place of god in the trilogy, see Bartlett 2016 on the *Theaetetus*, as well as Cropsey 1995, 61; Stern 2008, 130; and Zuckert 2009, 613–14.

critical sequels, Plato makes the *Theaetetus* complete the trilogy as its missing fourth, while allowing it to stand complete on its own.[37]

That the *Theaetetus* turns the trilogy into the anticipated tetralogy can be seen from a consideration of the contours that the Stranger has given his characterization of the diacritical core of statecraft. As an unraveling of the opinions that the laws have embedded in our souls, this diacritical core would expose the limited veracity of the city's education in virtue, so as to catch a glimpse of the true as opposed to apparent good. One discerns herein a version of Socratic refutation, and so the philosopher's apparition (φάντασμα) as a statesman. Would the Socrates of the *Theaetetus*—"the midwife who never lets the offspring he brings into light survive in the light of truth"—be the diacritical core of statecraft? A detail strengthens this suggestion. Within Plato's works but outside of the *Theaetetus*, midwifery is mentioned only once, specifically, in the discussion of herding in the *Statesman*.[38] There it is listed among the many tasks herders perform but which the statesman's sort of herding would leave for another (268b2). This apparently only passing mention is intriguing. How could anyone midwife a herd? One could do so only on a case-by-case basis. There is, then, a sort of nurturing of a herd akin to statecraft, but which *necessarily* occurs in

---

[37] On the illusory completeness of the *Theaetetus*, see Davis 2018a.—Klein concludes that Euclides must also have recorded the *Sophist* and *Statesman* (Klein 1977, 75). This would mean that Socrates also took the trouble to have these dialogues recorded. This view, proposed (according to Klein) by Munk 1857, 421, and considered also by Bartlett 2016, 226 n. 1, seems difficult to maintain, in light of Euclides' silence on at least the Stranger, if not also Young Socrates. His silence on Theodorus suggests he is unaware of the important role he plays in the dialogue, as discussed in Chapter IV.

[38] Zuckert, too, notes that Socratic widwifery is peculiar to the *Theaetetus* (Zuckert 2009, 608). Gwenda-lin Grewal has pointed out to me that the three waves (κύματα) of laughter in the *Republic* could also be pregnancies, so that Glaucon, Adeimantus, and Polemarchus forcibly induce labor in Socrates at the outset of Book V. In this case, it is Socrates who is pregnant, rather than his interlocutors; likewise, the birth seems forced rather than felicitous, which says quite a bit about the differences between the *Republic* and the *Theaetetus*.

private. And in its privacy, it wouldn't have much use for laws. That is, it would be more thoroughgoingly diacritical than the legislator-statesman could ever hope to be. Socrates's ironic guise as a midwife who only seems to deliver stillborn offspring seems to be the elusive, diacritical core of statecraft. Did Socrates learn his art from Phaenarete or Penelope?

In any case, the *Theaetetus* promises to pick up right where the *Statesman* left off.[39] We return to it, then, but now in full awareness of the Stranger's failed attempt to gratify Theodorus' annoyance with or even anger at Socrates (*Sophist* 216b7–c1). The *Sophist* and *Statesman* don't even appear to have been a deviation from the path that returns to the path (περίοδος) but rather a departure from the path that never takes us home but rather somewhere altogether new (διέξοδος) (277b2–3: τὸ τῆς ἔμπροσθεν ἁμάρτημα διεξόδου; see 279c5). Accordingly, we must read it not as we did before, through the eyes of Theodorus, but as Socrates wrote it, that is, in full awareness of Theodorus' misunderstanding of him and of the Stranger's exposition of that misunderstanding over the course of the *Sophist* and *Statesman*. We must read it as Socrates' imprisoned meditation on how and why he was destined to be thus misunderstood.

---

[39] As Benardete puts it, "weaving is doubly paradigmatic; it exemplifies at once *politikē* and *dialektikē*. The length of its account therefore is both too long and too short. It is too long if it were designed only to clarify *politikē*, and it is too short in its inability to display all of *dialektikē*" (Benardete 2000, 371). That longer application occurs, I maintain, in the *Theaetetus* as sequel to the *Statesman*.

IV

"THEAETETUS"

I.

In the chronology of Plato's dialogues, we expect that after the *Statesman* we will find the *Philosopher*. Instead, however, we encounter the *Apology of Socrates*, whose title appears to promise a suitable replacement.[1] Likewise promising is its content, for Socrates not only delivers a defense speech against the present accusation by Anytus, Meletus, and Lycon, but also gives an account of how he came by the wisdom that made him so famous or infamous (*Apology of Socrates* 20c4–d4). That is, he sets out to defend his life as a whole, the same life he summarized at the beginning of the *Sophist* and then invited the Stranger to critique. How could it *not* be the missing *Philosopher*? Troublingly, however, Socrates never explains how he got his initial reputation for wisdom—neither the wisdom of which his initial accusers spoke nor the wisdom that supposedly prompted Chaerephon to consult the oracle at Delphi (*Apology of Socrates* 18b4–c1, 21a4–6). Socrates is silent, it appears, because those listening either to the initial conversations that gave rise to the "accusation" that he is wise or to that "accusation" alone subsequently accused him of atheism, that is, of impiety (*Apology of Socrates* 18b4–c3, c3–4). And *this* accusation was then turned into an accusation also of injustice, from which arose the present indictment (*Apology of Socrates* 19b3–c2, 24b6–c1). Socrates' self-defense must therefore take the form of a defense *not* of his wisdom but of the justice and piety of his wisdom. Thus, in place of an account of how he came

---

[1] See note 11.

by his famous or infamous wisdom, Socrates gives us the story of his divine mission. Though he prefaces this story by saying he will attempt a demonstration (πειράσομαι ἀποδεῖξαι) of how he got his name or reputation (ὄνομα), he concludes rather that the god has used his name (τῷ ἐμῷ ὀνόματι) and made him a model (ἐμὲ παράδειγμα ποιούμενος), whom the youth in turn imitate (μιμοῦνται) (*Apology of Socrates* 20d2–4, 23a7–b4, c5). The language here recalls the *Statesman*, while suggesting the limitations of Socrates' present defense of his wisdom: compelled by his indictment to defend his way of life and to do so in the most public manner, Socrates offers a poetic distortion of himself in those terms most familiar to the city, in terms of justice and piety. It is for this reason, in part, that Socrates eventually defends himself as Athens' savior, as her strange new hero, the Achilles of wakeful rationality (*Apology of Socrates* 28b3–d4).[2]

---

[2] I qualify the above with "in part," because the situation is in reality quite a bit more complex. Though the putative nobility of Socrates' wisdom was implicit in his autobiography—specifically, in his commitment to his way of life despite the attendant risks—nevertheless that nobility remains underdeveloped until a hypothetical interlocutor asks him whether he's ashamed of running such risk of death (*Apology of Socrates* 28b3–5). Prior to this moment, the jurors have intervened only to compel Meletus to answer Socrates' questions; after, however, they intervene in protest of Socrates' comparison of himself to Achilles (*Apology of Socrates* 27b3–c5 with 30c3–5). The risk of death appears to have been minimized, so long as Socrates argued only for the piety and justice of his wisdom on the basis of his δαιμόνιον—that is, so long as he appeared just an oddball (see *Euthyphro* 3c6–d2). Accordingly, his way of life appeared peculiarly his own: "Let us…assume that the Platonic dialogues…present the Socratic way of life as a model. Yet they cannot tell us: live as Socrates lived. For Socrates' life was rendered possible by his possession of a 'demonic' gift and we do not possess such a gift" (Strauss 1964, 51). Only after Socrates has articulated the implications of this commitment by translating it into the Achillean model familiar to the Athenian jurors do they come to see that Socrates' way of life is not merely his own but rather imitable by others—particularly, by the youth (see *Apology of Socrates* 23c2–6).

In his trial, then, Socrates attempted to present his way of life as pious, just, and (eventually) noble so as to render it attractive to the city. Whether he intended that attraction to come as a result of an ennobling rhetoric or as a result of a noble death requires a thoroughgoing examination of his reasons for giving such a speech and for accepting its consequences; that is, it requires an interpretation of the *Apology of Socrates* and the *Crito*. This task would take us too far afield. Nevertheless, it can safely be said that of all of Socrates' *deeds*, he made none stand out more powerfully against the rest of his life, the whole of antiquity, and indeed human history since, than that of his death. But when it comes to his *speeches*, and which of them he left as a testament to his way of life, the Platonic Socrates took no pains to have any recorded save that found in the *Theaetetus*. This selection is all the more surprising, as it is this conversation that provoked, first, Theodorus' accusation against Socrates of being a sophist—albeit a peculiar one—and, second, his subsequent scientific trial at the hands of his judge, the Stranger. That is, it brought even the most scientific men into agreement with Socrates' accusers in consequence, if not also in principle. Nevertheless, as we have seen, though the bonds of guest-friendship (ξενία) with Theodorus compelled the Stranger to offer more conclusive results than he might have otherwise, nevertheless this judge's verdict stands with Socrates. And when we return to the *Theaetetus* with fresh eyes to reevaluate our initial, flawed reading, we see immediately that Socrates finds himself in a situation similar to that of the Stranger, when Theaetetus readily agrees to reduce wisdom (σοφία) to knowledge or science (ἐπιστήμη) (145e1–7).[3] Whereas in the *Apology of Socrates* Socrates was compelled to reduce wisdom to that portion of it that could be understood as pious and just, in the *Theaetetus* Socrates was compelled to reduce it to a science—to understand the word σοφία not in the highest sense of wisdom but

---

[3] Unless noted otherwise, all references in this chapter are to the *Theaetetus*.

in the broader sense of expertise.[4] The *Theaetetus* thus emerges as the scientific counterpart to the *Apology of Socrates*, as Socrates' response to the indictment of his way of life not as unjust and impious but as needlessly impure in its imprecision.

Socrates gets Theaetetus to agree to the identification of wisdom with knowledge by appealing to the sorts of subjects he learns (μανθάνεις) from Theodorus—subjects like astronomy, harmony, and calculations (λογισμούς) and about which Theaetetus says he is eager (προθυμοῦμαί γε δή) to learn (145c7–d3).[5] Socrates, too, finds himself eager about such matters, though he is also perplexed (ἀπορῶ) about something small that is to be examined—out of some unstated necessity—with both Theaetetus and those present (145d4–7).[6] The perplexity, it turns out, concerns the question, Whatever does knowledge happen to be?, but specifically in terms of the agreement that learning is becoming wiser concerning what one learns and the consequent identification of wisdom with scientific knowledge (ἐπιστήμη) (145d7–146a1). For elsewhere Socrates does not hesitate to define virtue as knowledge; indeed, he did so toward the end of his conversation with the living Protagoras some thirty years prior (*Protagoras* 360e6–361c2). Unfortunately, Protagoras preferred at this late stage in the conversation to cut his losses and cease conversing with Socrates rather than continue on and risk further embarrassment before potential students (*Protagoras* 361d7–e6). And though in *his* conversation with Socrates Theaetetus displays more good will than Protagoras, to say the least, nevertheless he is frozen in silence when Socrates initially poses the question of what knowledge is (145e8–146a5). Both men find themselves si-

---

[4] In Homer's time, σοφίη primarily meant expertise, a sense it retained even in Aristotle. See the entries for σοφία in Cunliffe 1963 and Liddell et al. 1996, as well as Burnyeat 1990, 19.

[5] On the *Theaetetus* as a challenging Theodorus' education of Theaetetus, see Zuckert 2009, 604–8.

[6] As with Socrates' use of σκεπτέον here, verbal adjectives with the -τεος ending denote necessity (see Smyth 1920, §358).

lenced by Socrates: Protagoras out of his jilted love of victory, Theaetetus out of his sense of inadequacy before the question. If Socrates is to keep Theaetetus engaged in conversation, he will have to persuade him of his ability to answer their question.

Initially, Theaetetus is urged on readily (146b1–c5). For he sees in his earlier discussion with Socrates—namely in the things one might learn from Theodorus—some examples of sciences (ἐπιστῆμαι), all and each of which are nothing else than (a) science (146c6–d3). He seems to have understood Socrates' question not as, Whatever does knowledge happen to be?, but as, Whatever happens to be a science?, both of which are possible translations of the Greek (ἐπιστήμη ὅτι ποτὲ τυγχάνει ὄν) (145e9–146a1; see *Hippias Major* 287d2–e4). Socrates clarifies that what he wants to know is, Whatever is knowledge itself? (ἐπιστήμην αὐτὸ ὅτι ποτ' ἐστίν) (146e7–10). In the course of their consideration of this more precise formulation of Socrates' question, Theaetetus recalls a recent experience during a conversation with Young Socrates (147c7–d2). Setting aside the details of the experience, we simply note that it involved their solving a problem concerning irrational magnitudes that had stumped their teacher Theodorus, a solution accomplished through an imaging (ἀπεικάσαντες) of these magnitudes in plane and solid figures (147c7–148b5).[7] In other words, Theaetetus evinces a willingness to engage in a didactic patricide and venture to comprehend irrational magnitudes—that is, the potentially limitless—through imagery. Strikingly, then, Theaetetus succeeds here where he failed in the *Sophist*, as there he was willing to defy the Stranger only to escape the sophist's limitless phantasms. For this reason, perhaps, Socrates tells Theaetetus and Young Socrates that they have done the best things human beings can do, so that Theodorus did not

---

[7] Howland also finds Theaetetus' uses of images important in its potential to serve as a model for Socrates' investigation of "the problem of human *dunamis*" (Howland 1998, 64).

bear false witness when praising Theaetetus' soul (148b4–5). Theaetetus thus appears well-poised to venture with Socrates into the unfamiliar waters before him.

Nevertheless, Theaetetus' eagerness (προθυμία), his courage and defiance, his willingness to think through the limitless by way of images is, as we noted in Chapter One, peculiarly circumscribed to mathematics. For he responds to Socrates by demurring about his ability to answer what Socrates asked about knowledge, defying him and discounting Theodorus' judgment only for the purpose of escaping the conversation altogether (148b6–c1). Theaetetus does with Socrates what he will do with the Stranger on the next day—rather, as he *did* with the Stranger prior to Socrates' later dictation of the conversation to Euclides. Socrates attempts to encourage Theaetetus by noting that a silver-medal-winning runner is not simply unskilled and that it is for the higher men to discover what knowledge is—indeed, Theaetetus adds, it is for the highest of all—so that Theaetetus should be bold and eager (προθυμήτητι) not just when it comes to mathematics but also when it comes to the question of what knowledge is (148c2–d2). And though Theaetetus notes his eagerness (προθυμίας), still when Socrates pivots (ἴθι δή) to ask again what knowledge is, Theaetetus once again demurs, but with greater explanation (148d3–7). "People have reported your questions to me," he says in effect. "And I myself have also attempted to articulate what knowledge is. But all I have found, Socrates, is that no one speaks adequately. I have therefore come to doubt my abilities, though despite all that my concern still abides" (see 148e1–6). Remarkably, Theaetetus has noticed—however faintly—the pervasive ignorance that Socrates noted at the outset of the *Sophist*, but also spoke of so eloquently and famously during his trial (see *Sophist* 216c2–d2, *Apology of Socrates* 22e1–23b4). Still, Theaetetus' reaction is to retreat, not to advance.[8] The Stranger was

---

[8] Benardete remarks that Theaetetus might have done well to generalize his list into a definition of science as "the knowledge of how to count and

careful to lead Theaetetus slowly into the problem of the sophist; Socrates, however, has instead thrown him into that now long-storied thicket, the question of what knowledge is. In the *Sophist*, the Stranger convinced Theaetetus that he was in good hands by posing as his guide through the forbidding terrain traversed during their hunt for the sophist. Confronted now with a Theaetetus whose lack of confidence in his abilities stands athwart his concern and eagerness, Socrates too must don a guise no less encouraging than that of the leader of the hunt—perhaps a still more encouraging one.

Toward that end, Socrates interprets the tension in Theaetetus' soul as the mark *not* of a desire tragically destined to remain unsatisfied but of a burgeoning potential—a pregnancy, as it were—with Socrates being the indispensable agent of actualization—a midwife, he says. It cannot be denied that Socrates' ironic guise as a midwife is successful in encouraging Theaetetus, as the youth responds both by noting his eagerness (προθυμεῖσθαι) and by offering a definition (151d7–e3). The success is owed in large part to Socrates' explanation to Theaetetus that the tension he senses in his soul is the birth pang of perplexity (ἀπορίας ἐμπίμπλανται) (151a5–b1). It is just this habit of making (ποιῶ) people perplexed (ἀπορεῖν) that Theaetetus has heard about Socrates from others (149a6–b1). Aided by Socrates' "midwifery," then, Theaetetus might finally give birth to a bouncing baby truth. Such is the hope, at least. Yet it is peculiar that Socrates refers to perplexity as birth pangs, since his conversation with Theaetetus began with Socrates' confession to his own perplexity about what knowledge is (145d5–7, 145e8–146a1). How can Socrates claim to be sterile of wisdom (ἄγονός…σοφίας) when he experiences the very pangs that in Theaetetus evince pregnancy? Is Socrates really a midwife to pregnant boys, or does he impregnate

---

measure" (Benardete 2000, 302). Such a move would have changed the dialogue dramatically: "Had Theaetetus given the answer we expect, he would have shown his daring in extending what he knows into all that he does not know and claiming thereby that whatever is not countable or measurable is not knowledge" (Benardete 2000, 302). This is the position Young Socrates favors in the *Statesman* (see Chapter III, Section II beginning).

them with perplexities?[9] Indeed, is it not precisely this habit of passing on his perplexity that earned him his indictment (*Apology of Socrates* 23c2–e3; see *Meno* 79e7–80b7 with 94e3–95a1)? In confirmation of this suspicion, Socrates admits that his midwifery differs from the usual sort inasmuch as occasionally the child birthed may not be true but rather an image (εἴδωλον) and that the disposal of this faux child risks arousing the mother's indignation (151b8–c7). A quick gloss of the dialogues readily shows that the child birthed is less often hallowed than hollowed—certainly it is of the latter and not the former that Theaetetus has heard reports (149a1–b1). That is, Socrates deceptively softens Theaetetus' fear that Socrates' much-discussed questioning does not resolve perplexity but rather culminates in it. Likewise, Socrates also speaks as though oblivious of the Stranger's division of spoken images (εἴδωλα λεγόμενα) into apparitions (φαντάσματα) and semblances (εἰκόνες), and thus the eventual problem of acquiring the dialectical science. These details thus serve as premonitions of the challenges that await Theaetetus—that, contrary to our initial reading, these challenges await *him* and not Socrates.

So, at the same time as Socrates promises to deliver from Theaetetus a true offspring in the form of a definition of knowledge, he suggests that this true offspring will be a perplexity rather than a true opinion. That is, Socrates affirms, however quietly, the Stranger's understanding of being as "impassable species" (ἄπορον εἶδος) or "essential perplexity." Consequently, the conditions under which Theaetetus will remain in the conversation are at odds with the conditions under which he might arrive at an understanding of the problem of knowledge. As the conversation unfolds, Socrates will have to navigate this strait, avoiding the twin pitfalls of dogmatically affirming and aggressively refuting Theaetetus' definitions. In the first half of the dialogue, Socrates risks discouraging Theaetetus altogether in his attempt to defeat Protagoras, whose

---

[9] Many have dwelled on the inconsistencies in Socrates' "self-portrait" as a midwife. For the most concise account, see Benardete 2018, 303–4.

thought guides Theaetetus' first definition of knowledge as perception (151e1–152a1). But, as we will see, Socrates' "midwifery" succeeds in encouraging Theaetetus, so much so that immediately after Socrates refutes the first definition Theaetetus offers up a second (186e9–187a8).[10] Consequently, the first half of the dialogue is not, as we surmised in Chapter One, Socrates' attempt to distinguish himself from Protagoras, but rather Socrates' demonstration of his deep agreement with Protagoras as to the necessity of using the apparition-making art (φανταστική) (Section II). A correlative reversal occurs in the second half of the dialogue, which no longer shows Socrates collapsing, against his will, with Protagoras, but rather illustrates how Socratic refutation is an apparition-making that rises to the level of a semblance-making art (εἰκαστική). So understood, Socrates' self-presentation in the *Theaetetus* constitutes an examination of the diacritical core of statecraft (Section III). It thus prepares us to survey the entirety of the preceding terrain, so as to grasp what the philosopher is, in relation to the sophist and statesman, and thus how Socrates might respond to his modern and contemporary accusers (Section IV).

II.

In our first reading of the *Theaetetus*, the dialogue appeared as a tragedy in two acts, the first of which featured Socrates' exposition and examination of Theaetetus' first definition of knowledge. In Scene One, Socrates raised Protagoras to new heights, while Scene Two saw them in a dialectical swordfight. Viewed through the lens of Socrates' ironic guise as a midwife, however, Scene One changes character altogether, for it is not only Protagoras who is raised to

---

[10] "By presenting himself as an intellectual midwife, Socrates tries literally to *en*-courage Theaetetus to submit to the questions he fears he cannot answer by promising to help him through a painful process that will relieve him in the end of his perplexity" (Zuckert 2009, 612).

new heights, but Theaetetus as well. Socrates' practice of "midwifery" expands the usually brief, initial stage of a conversation—the giving of a definition—into a much longer process, in which the virtues of that definition are elaborated by situating it in a larger context. In the case of Theaetetus' definition of knowledge as perception, this involves developing the definition into a thoroughgoing ontology—or, rather, anti-ontology (see 157b1). Whereas with Theaetetus' first attempt at a definition—his list of sciences—the first stage took just five lines (146c7–d3), with the first definition proper it takes more than ten Stephanus pages—and that's excluding Socrates' three-page discussion of his "midwifery," necessary for convincing Theaetetus to provide a definition at all (151d7–160e5, 148e7–151d6). As we will see, in this respect and others, what appeared to be part of the tragedy of Socrates was in reality part of Socrates' encouragement of Theaetetus. Correspondingly, it will concern not the disagreement between Socrates and Protagoras but their deep agreement, namely, as to the necessity of using an art of distortive apparitions (φανταστική). As we will see, the philosophic education of Theaetetus is impossible without the philosopher's sophistic self-distortion as a midwife.

It isn't difficult to see how the delivery portion of Socrates' "midwifery" gives Theaetetus greater confidence. Socrates initially responds by praising Theaetetus for speaking well and nobly (151e4). He then connects Theaetetus' definition with the thought of Protagoras, whom he calls a wise man (σοφὸν ἄνδρα) (151e8–152b1; compare *Sophist* 216a4). It turns out that Theaetetus keeps still more illustrious company than this, as Socrates also places him in the camp of all the wise men, including Heraclitus, Empedocles, Epicharmus, and Homer—all, that is, save father Parmenides (152e1–8). Backed by so great an army with so eminent a poet as Homer for its general, Theaetetus now doubts that *anyone*—himself included—could contend against a definition that just moments earlier he had been reluctant even to utter (153a1–4). Offering up further indications of the strength of his thesis, Socrates discusses how motion is responsible for generation, that it maintains both body and soul and, indeed, even does so on a cosmic level (153a5–d7). He likewise continues developing Theaetetus' definition into a robust, relativist account of the relationship between man and world, according to which account everyone is equal in point of knowledge (153e4–154a9, 155d9–157d12, 158e5–160d4). At the same time, however, Socrates develops the uneasy relationship between the Protagorean thesis and Theaetetus' conviction that mathematics and its kindred sciences produce knowledge over and against ignorance (154b1–155c7, 157e1–158e4). Socrates is thus able to heighten the tension in Theaetetus' soul, so that he is not even one with himself (154a6–9). But even here Socrates finds cause to praise Theaetetus, as the elder Athenian proclaims the youth's wonder and perplexity as evidence of his philosophic nature (155c8–d8). Socrates can thus close the delivery section by praising Theaetetus' definition as spoken entirely beautifully (παγκάλως), emphasizing again the illustrious company he keeps (160d5–e2). So impressive has Theaetetus' definition now become that his teacher Theodorus, otherwise reluctant to get involved, now bursts in of his own accord to praise Theaetetus' nature (161a5–6).

It is important not just to *note*, as in Chapter One, but also to *emphasize* that Protagoras' thesis threatens not just Theaetetus' mathematical studies but Socrates' ignorance as well—his so-called sterility (ἀγνοία, ἀγονία) as a midwife. Protagoras can only demote Theaetetus' science by promoting Socrates to knower. They thus find themselves on opposite sides of the same perplexity. For Theaetetus, the Protagorean thesis renders the madman equal to the scientist. For Socrates, however, the problem is rather that he is forced to be a knower, when perhaps he senses he is closer rather to the madman (157e1–158e4; see *Sophist* 216d1–2, 242a10–b2). It is certainly peculiar to resist being called competent (see *Apology of Socrates* 22e1–6). To escape this dilemma, Theaetetus must find a firmer basis for scientific knowledge, such that the perceptions and claims of the mad and the ignorant may be dispelled. But for Socrates, escape will come rather by grounding his ignorance in the very nature of things, even in the absence of a standard for scientifically precise knowledge. And for this, Protagoras' thesis is in many ways quite helpful, as his identification of "being" with the momentary interplay of agent (τὸ ποιοῦν) and patient (τὸ πάσχον) proves an incredibly apt description of Socrates' irony, that is, his peculiar use of the apparition-making art (φανταστική): Socrates "is" a midwife, only insofar as he comes into contact with someone of Theaetetus' character. Indeed, the same was the case with the Stranger in the *Sophist* and *Statesman* (see Chapter III, Section IV, second paragraph). But to rescue his ignorance, Socrates necessarily risks discouraging Theaetetus. For this reason, the encouragement of Theaetetus, the first stage of which was the delivery of the first definition into a sophisticated account of man and world, is absolutely necessary to convincing him of the goodness of perplexity, of his wonder—of showing him the choice-worthiness of Socratic ignorance.

Encouraging Theaetetus during the delivery was in many ways an easy task, as Socrates needed only to engage in what could justly be called a form of flattery. But now that they find themselves in the second stage, that of testing, the obstacle is quite great. For if Socrates rushes too quickly to the refutation, he risks discouraging Theaetetus altogether. Whereas other characters in the dialogues react to Socrates with frustration and anger, Theaetetus' reaction to Socrates' refutation of his list of sciences as a definition was to express a universal skepticism. That is, being refuted regarding what knowledge is corresponds entirely to his judgment that no one can speak sufficiently about it, himself included. Though Theodorus gives Theaetetus a vote of confidence, Theaetetus finds himself easily and unfathomably pulled in opposite directions (161a5–6, 162c7–d2: Μὰ Δί' οὐκ ἔγωγε; see, again, *Sophist* 216d1–2, 242a10–b2). That is, Theaetetus is still passive at the beginning of the testing or refutation section, even though he will by its end readily offer up a second definition. Against all odds, then, Socrates does manage to make refutation encouraging for Theaetetus. Even more remarkably, however, Socrates encourages Theaetetus while hardly speaking to him at all: though the testing takes some twenty-six Stephanus pages (161a6–187a3), Theaetetus drops out of the conversation altogether for some seventeen pages (165e8–183c7). What's more, it's in these seventeen pages that Theaetetus appears to undergo his change: Socrates brings Theodorus into the conversation citing the seriousness that comes with age, as opposed to the childish fear that impairs Theaetetus' judgment; by the end, however, the youthful Theaetetus interrupts the conversation to question his elders, as Theodorus himself notes with surprise, and even take their place, despite Socrates' reputation (168c6–e3, 183c4–d9). Somehow, then, during these seventeen pages, in which Theaetetus is completely silent, Socrates manages to get Theaetetus to commit didactic patricide *outside* of mathematics. What exactly happens to him during these seventeen pages, silently yet decisively?

As soon as Socrates has finished delivering Theaetetus' first offspring, he shifts his efforts to getting Theodorus involved. One suspects that it's not just what Socrates and Theodorus discuss, then, that effects this change in Theaetetus, but something about Theodorus himself. This suspicion is readily confirmed. Most conspicuously, Socrates takes no trouble to involve Theodorus in his conversation with Theaetetus either before or after this section of the dialogue. That is, Theodorus' involvement appears necessary, despite his minimal contributions, to this particular section of the dialogue. More pointedly, it is peculiar that Socrates even takes as long as he does to dismiss the first definition, since Theaetetus very early on touches upon the sort of observation on which Socrates' final argument against Protagoras will rely (163a7–c6, 186d2–5; consider, too, 163c5 with 148b4).[11] As soon as Theaetetus does so, Socrates praises him, only to distract him immediately thereafter with a second consideration (163c6–8). Like the Stranger in the *Sophist*, Socrates introduces a long digression unnecessary to the argument yet apparently, as we will see, for pedagogical purposes. When Socrates eventually returns to Theaetetus' observation, Theodorus will have

---

[11] Note that Theaetetus invokes the standard of expertise: οἵ τε γραμματισταὶ περὶ αὐτῶν καὶ οἱ ἑρμηνῆς διδάσκουσιν (163c2–3).

exited the conversation, and this time for good. Theodorus' involvement thus proves unnecessary even for the most substantive portion of the argument. That is, he seems more important in terms of his character than in terms of any knowledge of Protagoras' thought that he might possess—even though this is the pretense under which Socrates brings Theodorus into the discussion. But how could Theaetetus' character stand to improve in silent observation of Theodorus, a man uninterested in the topics under consideration, averse to philosophic discourse generally, and, to be blunt, ridiculous in his cowardly protests? How could he be anything but a *negative* example, despite Socrates' explicit statements to the contrary?

Now, Theodorus initially cites his friendship with Protagoras and his stiffness from old age as preventing his involvement in the conversation (162a4–b9). In response, Socrates returns to Theaetetus, who confesses his confusion with and susceptibility to changes in the argument (162c7–d2). Speaking as Protagoras, Socrates chastises himself for presenting arguments that fall short of the geometers' rigorous standards of demonstration (ἀπόδειξιν) and necessity (ἀνάγκην) (162d3–163a1). Socrates further portrays himself as declaring victory too quickly, as though himself inadequate in stating Protagoras' view in a manner faithful to the man himself; as it stands, they are guilty of abusing Protagoras' orphaned thought (164b8–e7). Implicitly, then, Socrates erects a standard for the ideal interlocutor, a geometer well-acquainted both with Protagoras' thought and the man himself. When Socrates invokes this standard to bring Theodorus into the conversation, Theodorus deflects, saying that not he but Callias is the orphan's guardian (164e8–165a3). And though Theodorus does agree to join Theaetetus by overseeing his answers, he drops his involvement after their first cooperative reply (165a4–c3, esp. c3: φήσω οἶμαι). In response, Socrates again imitates Protagoras and in this guise offers his most robust defense of Protagoras' thought, at the same time chastising Socrates (himself, that is) for taking advantage of the fear of a mere child, Theaetetus, so as to win victory in the absence of rigorous demonstration

(165e8–168c5). By assuming the responsibility of expounding Protagoras' thought, Socrates absolves Theodorus of having to do so himself, while further elaborating his standard for the ideal interlocutor into an *old* geometer well-acquainted with Protagoras himself. Socrates' tactic finally wins Theodorus over, as he is now so impressed with Socrates' work that he cannot help but acknowledge the standard Socrates has erected (168c6–169c7).[12]

Socrates' standard no doubt moves Theaetetus, too, for he is effectively told that he needs to grow up, that he must overcome his childish fear and become a man. At the same time, however, we cannot help but find Theodorus still more defective than Theaetetus. Though Theaetetus required the encouragement of Socrates' "midwifery" to get him involved, Theodorus needed still more; though Theaetetus seems lacking in confidence, Theodorus seems afraid of embarrassment before his students. Theodorus fails to see that a teacher fearful of looking ridiculous before his students only risks looking more ridiculous before the best of them. And it is precisely this failure that Socrates exploits to Theaetetus' benefit. Initially, Theodorus enters the conversation on the condition that he will be released once Protagoras' thought has been thoroughly examined and, as he surmises, refuted (168c8–e3 with 169c4–7). Along the way, however, they agree that thoroughness *also* dictates that they treat both the Heracliteans, among whom he counts Protagoras, and the Parmenideans (180d7–181b7). But because they discuss and dispose of the Heracliteans prior to turning to the Parmenideans, Theodorus has fulfilled the first agreement without yet fulfilling the second.[13] The conflict between their two agreements

---

[12] Others have noted this tactic: "By having Protagoras object first to him frightening a mere child, Socrates begins his defense by laying the grounds for his later insistence that Theodorus come to the assistance of his friend" (Zuckert 2009, 620).

[13] Some have found Socrates' connection of Theaetetus' Protagorean definition with Heraclitus suspicious, including Burnyeat 1990, 7–10 and Stern 2008, 82. Benardete sees the solution as residing in a revision of Socratic maieutics into erotics: "Theaetetus's definition, which appeared as one, now

thus gives Theodorus an opportunity to back out of a conversation he never wanted in on in the first place, while giving Theaetetus an opportunity to hold his teacher accountable to what philosophic thoroughness demands. It doesn't help Theodorus' chances of getting out of the conversation early that, along the way, Socrates takes a digression on the philosopher, whose freedom and leisure, we recall, allow him to tailor his speeches to being itself rather than to fleeting exigencies. That is, not only does Socrates offer Theaetetus a standard by which to judge philosophic thoroughness, he also magnifies that standard into a full-fledged image of the free and leisurely philosopher. Theodorus does indeed serve as a negative example, then, but in light of the positive standard of philosophic freedom and leisure. This pairing succeeds in moving Theaetetus, as he will soon explicitly and of his own accord invoke this standard (187d9–11). Noticing a gap between an ideal he shares with his teacher and his teacher's actual conduct, Theaetetus accomplishes in his discussion of knowledge what he had done recently in mathematics: a didactic patricide. Unlike the Stranger's digression, Socrates' actually achieves something.

Socrates thus succeeds where the Stranger failed, and quite impressively: after the delivery, Theodorus chimed in because he was so impressed with Theaetetus' performance; by the end of their testing of the first definition, Theaetetus has questioned Theodorus' judgment, disposed of a definition that put him in the company of Homer and his ilk, and not hesitated to offer a second definition of his own in its place. Strange though it may seem, Socrates' "midwifery" does succeed in making Theaetetus somewhat more manly. In these seventeen pages, then, Socrates gives Theaetetus a model to imitate, effectively offering him the consolation of a good nature

---

comes to light as having concealed a two—Protagoras and Heraclitus—who have come together to produce Theaetetus' definition," but in reality "Socrates and Theaetetus…have engendered together Theaetetus's thesis": "Socrates and Theaetetus are a couple" (Benardete 2000, 307, 320). See, also, note 19.

should his definition eventually undergo refutation. Indeed, by embracing such refutation, Theaetetus will only confirm for himself his philosophic freedom to take the time necessary to tailor his speeches to being. In one respect, Socrates' tactic is successful, as Theaetetus shows enthusiasm in shifting his conception of knowledge from the passivity of perception to the more active process of a gathering-together (συλλογισμός) or gathering-up (ἀναλογισμός) in relation to our perceptions. In another respect, however, Socrates still has some way to go, as Theaetetus identifies this active process with the more passive reception of a seeming (δοκεῖ εἶναι) and its active transformation into discourse as an opinion (δόξα)—in the case of knowledge, as Theaetetus immediately clarifies, a *true* opinion (187a7–8: δοξάζειν with b4–8: ἡ ἀληθὴς δόξα). This second definition thus appears to be the offspring of Socratic activity and Theaetetan passivity. Indeed, it appears to reflect Theaetetus' hope that Socrates' "midwifery" might result in truth, as opposed to a falsity or image. The second definition is thus an apparition (φάντασμα) that draws the sleepy Theaetetus out of his mathematical cave and toward the wakefulness and light of Socratic knowledge of ignorance. But this is only possible if Socrates' particular practice of making distortive apparitions (φανταστική) is at the same time the making of accurate semblances (εἰκαστική); that remains to be seen.

III.

According to our tragic reading of the *Theaetetus* in Chapter One, Socrates' treatment of Theaetetus' first definition featured the elder Athenian's revivification of and dialectical battle with the long-dead Protagoras. Read through the lens of Socrates' "midwifery," however, it has emerged rather as the demonstration of the deep agreement between Protagoras and Socrates as to the necessity of using an art of making distortive apparitions (φανταστική).[14] Viewed thus, Socrates' behavior during the first half of the dialogue took on a new significance, inasmuch as it turned out to be necessary for encouraging Theaetetus. Even Socrates' initially off-putting hounding of Theodorus—the very hounding that inclined the elder mathematician to bring the Stranger to correct Socrates' conduct—was indispensable to showing Theaetetus how his skepticism, grounded as it is in fear, is not the product of philosophic freedom but a failure to live up to it. As we will presently see, the remainder of the *Theaetetus* undergoes a correlative transformation. Socrates' treatment of Theaetetus' second definition of knowledge as true opinion immediately raises the question of how false opinion is possible, a question that appeared to challenge Socratic philosophy at its root. For if false opinion isn't possible, how can Socrates claim that he might deliver from Theaetetus a truth as opposed to a falsity or image? Viewed in this light, Socrates' shift from the three logical definitions of false opinion to the two analogical definitions signaled the beginning of his tragic fall, with the Stranger's distinction of spoken images (εἴδωλα λεγόμενα) into distortive apparitions (φαντάσματα) and accurate semblances (εἰκόνες) the first step in escaping Socrates' fate. Now, however, Socrates' shift from the logical to the analogical appears rather as a rise, inasmuch as that shift signals an increased awareness of the problem images pose to thinking, the very subject of the *Sophist*. Accordingly, we are brought deeper into Socrates' use of apparitions. And what we will see is that, far from Socrates collapsing with Protagoras, as we concluded

---

[14] "Socrates, at least as Plato presents him, clearly understood that the greatest things at the very least must be approached through *phantastic* images…Thus in the *Republic*, Socrates offers the sun as a *phantastic* image of the good; in the *Phaedrus* he offers the image of the charioteer and the black and white horse as an image of the soul; in the *Crito* he personifies the laws and makes them speak; and so forth. In each of the cases mentioned, as in many others, what is being presented imagistically or phantastically is some *idea*" (Speliotis 2013, 209).

in Chapter One, Socrates' examination of Theaetetus' final two definitions will show how Socratic apparition-making (φανταστική) is at the same time a semblance-making (εἰκαστική).

The major premise of the discussion of false opinion is that, concerning everything and with respect to each individually, one either knows or doesn't know them (188a1–2). Socrates thus sets aside learning and forgetting "at present" (ἐν τῷ παρόντι), since they're between knowing and not knowing (188a2–4). This exclusion is justified (γὰρ), Socrates argues, because learning and forgetting are of no relation to their account at present (νῦν...ἡμῖν πρὸς λόγον ἐστὶν οὐδέν) (188a4). Socrates thus suggests that, at a different time, with a different interlocutor, or under a different argument, knowledge might not exclude ignorance but somehow be coextensive with it.[15] Indeed, he seems to suggest that such a combination would give rise to another opposition, namely, between learning (μανθάνειν) and forgetting (ἐπιλανθάνεσθαι). Socrates quietly introduces this opposition as he shifts from the logical to analogical definitions, since in the latter he concerns himself with the coming-into-being (γένεσις) of true and false opinions, that is, the motion or activity leading to such results. Likewise, when Socrates presents the final image—that of the soul as a dovecote—he expands upon this intellectual motion, with knowledge appearing to be a sort of bird, whose nature is discerned not in possession, as they anticipate, but in pursuit—in how it tends to this gathering or that (see 197d8–10). Socrates' slide across his five proposals suggests that knowledge is an activity or motion rather than a static condition of soul. And, moreover, it suggests a connection with the Stranger's implicit understanding of being as impassable species or essential perplexity (ἄπορον εἶδος). For only if being is somehow impassable would knowledge and ignorance collapse and the decisive matter be our disposition or activity in relation to our ignorance rather than the purity of the outcome of a thought process. By framing the question

---

[15] For a detailed examination of this possibility as a solution to the problem of false opinion, see Bolotin 1987.

of knowledge in terms of the activity and passivity of the soul—as though what is to be avoided is not ignorance as such but a tendency toward passive forgetfulness thereof—Socrates collapses the argument of the dialogue with its action, as the very activity of the soul he seeks to induce in Theaetetus appears to be that combination of knowledge and ignorance referred to simply as learning. That is, Socrates must direct Theaetetus from lessons to be learned (τὰ μαθήματα) to active learning (μάθησις).

Socrates' refutation of Theaetetus' second definition continues the above tendency by prompting Theaetetus to adopt philosophy's high ambitions. Socrates accomplishes this by invoking, as we saw in Chapter One, the imagery from the digression on the high-flying philosopher. Specifically, he mentions again the water-clock, under whose pressure rhetoricians and jurists speak; in these circumstances, Socrates points out, one often finds people persuaded of a true opinion though they lack knowledge of the matter itself (201a7–b4, with 172d9–e4). With his second definition thus dismissed, Theaetetus is reminded that the philosopher's freedom from fleeting exigencies grants him the leisure necessary for tailoring his speeches to being, for arriving at true opinions with the demonstrative certainty of Theaetetus' own science of geometry. It is in this context that Theaetetus proposes his third and final definition of knowledge as a true opinion with an account (λόγος) (201c7–d3). As noted, this definition reflects the model of a Euclidean proof: an opinion is given in the form of "I say that…" and followed by an argument (λόγος) establishing its veracity. At the same time, however, Theaetetus shows that he has adopted Socrates' ambition, inasmuch as the definition extends this model to all things to be known. Theaetetus' final definition thus appears to be the offspring generated when one mates Socrates' ambition with Theaetetus' affinity for mathematics: like those before it, the final definition is an apparition (φάντασμα). Socrates seems to have been successful in transforming Theaetetus from an isolationist to an imperialist mathematician. He suggests as much in his elaboration of Theaetetus' definition, during which he refers to him who possesses such knowledge as having become perfect and complete with respect to knowledge (τελείως πρὸς ἐπιστήμην), an allusion back to Young Socrates' expectations of his and the Stranger's search for the statesman (202c5; see *Statesman* 267c4–d2, 277a1–2, 311c8–10). To transform this distortive apparition (φάντασμα) into an accurate semblance (εἰκών), Socrates will have to show the limits of fulfilling this ambition; but in dashing Theaetetus' expectations, Socrates necessarily risks driving Theaetetus back into the arms of Protagorean relativism. Nevertheless, Socrates has taken such pains to encourage him that Theaetetus might rather be poised to find some victory in the refutation of his third and final definition. It is through this refutation that Socrates will induce a perplexity in Theaetetus' apparition. Will he thereby somehow transform it into a semblance? That is, does the refutation of an apparition somehow transform it into a semblance of being, that is, of being as impassable, as essential perplexity (ἄπορον εἶδος)?

To answer this question, we must take greater care than we did in Chapter One when assessing the next passage, the passage in which we encounter what we have called the dilemma of intelligibility. It is worth rehearsing it in detail, as it takes on a new significance in light of the ontological passages from the *Sophist* and *Statesman*. Socrates makes a distinction between the intelligible things (τὰ ἐπιστητά) and the unintelligible things (τὰ μὴ ἐπιστητά), that is, being is such that in certain cases to be also means to be knowable (201d2–5). Socrates elaborates on Theaetetus' vague recollection with what he calls a dream, according to which the ultimate elements (στοιχεῖα) of things are so simple as to be unintelligible and only nameable; only the compounds woven (πέπλεκται) from these elements can be spoken, when we likewise weave their names together (συμπλακέντα) into a speech (λόγος) (201d6–202b8). In cases where we lack this speech, we opine truly but do not have knowledge; but when we do have it we are perfect in point of knowledge (τελείως πρὸς ἐπιστήμην ἔχειν) (202b8–c6). With this standard of perfection in place, Socrates introduces the aforementioned dilemma of intelligibility, which runs as follows.

A compound is either all the elements or some one look that comes into being when they are set together (203c3–6). Assuming it is all the elements, he who knows each of two elements is agreed to know both; but it is uncanny and startling (δεινὸν, ἐξαίφνης) to think that someone can know both elements while knowing neither of the two (203c7–e1). Thus, the compound isn't all the elements. They consider next, therefore, that it is some one look (ἰδέα) that comes into being when all the elements are set together (203e2–204a4). This brings them to the following question. How do we mean look (ἰδέα)? Is it a whole of parts, or is it indivisibly one? If it is a whole of parts, then the whole is either all the parts—so that the compound would, again, be all the elements and thus unknowable—or some look (εἶδος) other than all its parts (204a5–10). But it is agreed that, just as with "four plus two" or "three plus three" the whole "six" is all the elements, so too is every whole—Socrates uses the example of an army—all the parts (204a11–205a7). Thus, again, the whole is all the elements and, again, unknowable (205a8–b13, esp. b8–13). The only remaining option is that the compound is "some one, indivisible look" (μία τις ἰδέα ἀμέριστος) (205c1–3). But that just makes the compound as one as each of the elements, and so again unknowable (205c4–e5). In this way, the dilemma of intelligibility startlingly disrupts Theaetetus' dream: nothing, it turns out, can be known.

Now, we noted in Chapter One that the above argument relies on the assumption that, with respect to each thing, the entire number (ὁ...ἀριθμὸς πᾶς) is the entire being (τὸ ὂν πᾶν) (204d10–11); we noted, too, that this assumption reflected the seriousness of Socrates' audience of mathematicians—Theaetetus, Theodorus, and the rest—for whom mathematics provides the model for knowledge and so numbers the model for the beings. Now that we are free of the constraints of Theodorus' seriousness, however, we can submit this assumption to some examination. This assumption is introduced through a series of examples. The first example is the number six, for which this assumption is relatively unproblematic (204b10–d3). The second example—or, rather, pair of examples—are the

Greek measures of the πλέθρον and, more interestingly, the στάδιον, which is both a race-course and the measure of that race-course, that is, both a number and a thing (204d4–8). The third and most controversial example is the army. It is controversial because the army is most an army when in battle, and when in battle its number is constantly changing: the whole Athenian army did not dissipate simply because Theaetetus was removed from battle (204d9–12 with 142a6–b8). Rather, the whole army emerges out of a certain arrangement of the supra-elemental parts and the activity of their various functions. Indeed, the army ceases to be an army only when its ranks are broken or its guiding principle destroyed (consider Herodotus, *Histories* 7.224–25 with 9.62–64). Socrates' examples appear to work as a slippery slope, intended to convince Theaetetus that each and every thing is its number. In addition, Socrates facilitates Theaetetus' slide down this slippery slope by giving the whole and all the parts identical, negative definitions, namely, as that from which nothing is absent or missing (205a1–7: ὅταν μηδὲν ἀπῇ and οὗ ἂν μηδαμῇ μηδὲν ἀποστατῇ). Nevertheless, Socrates' approach could also be understood as attempting to introduce Theaetetus to that aspect of being which is not simply enumerable, which cannot simply be counted as one's fingers and toes.[16] This ambiguity in Socrates' intention is settled, I believe, by his prior encouragement of Theaetetus—an encouragement that resulted in an act of didactic parricide—and his increasing emphasis, more recently, on knowledge as an activity. This alone should have given Theaetetus pause about accepting so readily such a Theodoran interpretation of being. Indeed, had Socrates' argument *not* taken the form of a slippery slope, he would have made Theaetetus' patricide too rote, too passive, and so robbed him of its didactic benefits.

---

[16] Stern puts it most succinctly: "just so far as our knowing is faithful to the complexity of these wholes it falls short of the apodeictic certainty for which Theaetetus yearns. For this reason, here as elsewhere in the dialogue, Socrates makes the guiding question of their discussion not the possibility of certain knowledge but the possibility of learning, of inquiry" (Stern 2008, 258).

What should have been a challenge to Socrates' command of the argument—a challenge borne of genuine insight into a difference in kind between numbers and wholes—would have instead been just another routine affirmation of Socrates' understanding of things. That Theaetetus does not challenge the assumption that, with respect to each thing, the entire number is the entire being—especially after such long and careful encouragement from Socrates—constitutes his chief failure in this dialogue.[17] Though Socrates far exceeded the Stranger in bringing Theaetetus to challenge his attachment to an arithmetical understanding of being, still neither accomplishes a wholesale conversion to Socratic philosophy. That, it would seem, remains for another day.[18]

Theaetetus' failure to challenge his arithmetical understanding of being—to question his dream of being "perfect in point of knowledge"—is, in one respect, quite large. For it was this very demand that the thing known be known precisely, in the sense of one, that tripped up Socrates himself as a youth in the *Parmenides* (*Parmenides* 133a8–134e8). And what the aged Parmenides showed the young Socrates was that what is one and in no way many cannot be spoken of or known—we cannot even say or know that it is or that it is one (*Parmenides* 137c4–5, 141e9–142b3). Rather, whatever is knowable must be both one and many, a whole of parts, and whatever is a whole of parts must, to have parts, be other than itself and, to be a whole, be the same as itself (*Parmenides* 142b3–147c8, 155d3–e3). That is, it must be both unified with and contrary to itself, so that our speech about it is necessarily riddled with contradictions. Intelligibility thus entails contradiction, such that whatever is known is known only as a perplexity. Perplexity, in turn, only emerges out of the refutation of a particular opinion—whether it

---

[17] *Contra* Benardete 2000, 315.

[18] Perhaps this is why Socrates was so willing to have Euclides write the *Theaetetus* down, since Socrates' days were numbered. "Does Socrates' willingness to supplement Euclides' memory indicate that he changed his mind about the value of writing when he saw himself nearing death?" (Zuckert 2009, 598; see, also, 620)

comes from time immemorial or from a merely partial experience; but for this very reason, too, it is difficult to respond to the skeptic, who sees in such contradiction not the grounds for Socratic knowledge of ignorance but an inescapable and thus lamentable imprecision. In this respect, the young Socrates' education in the *Parmenides* produces the mature Socrates we know well from the other dialogues, that is, the Socrates who sees refutation and education as going hand-in-hand—not because the former is prefatory to the latter, but because they are identical. This is only to say that aspects of the philosopher's activity are easily mistaken for sophistry or statecraft—as refutation for refutation's sake or as a purifying and ennobling education fit even for the Great King of Persia. Theaetetus' error thus robs him of an insight that, properly understood, would have made him not just *look* like Socrates but also *be* like him. It is no small loss. But in another respect it is not so large as it appears. For, if perplexity only emerges out of the refutation of a particular opinion, then we cannot expect the same result for Theaetetus—a talented mathematician who is peculiarly sheepish outside his studies—and the young Socrates—a budding philosopher concerned with the reputation of philosophy among non-philosophers, with securing the basic premises of speech, be it everyday or philosophical (*Parmenides* 128a4–130a2). Whereas Parmenides left the young Socrates perplexed about whether man can have access to such precise beings as would allow for wholly competent rule, Socrates must leave Theaetetus perplexed about whether man can be perfect in point of knowledge, regardless of others. Similar those these perplexities may be, still they reflect quite different starting points.

Pivoting from his own question, Socrates returns to Theaetetus' third definition of knowledge as a true opinion with an account (λόγος), which relies on an account of being that is, as we observed in Chapter One, familiar from his own studies (see 201c7–d3). But in light of what we have learned from the *Statesman* in Chapter Three, we now notice that Socrates presents Theaetetus with a version of the ontology of method. Guided by this ontology—according to which the elements are more knowable than their compounds, which grow increasingly difficult to understand—Socrates turns to consider, then reject three proposals for what an account (λόγος) adds to a true opinion so as to make it knowledge.

The first understanding of that account is that it makes one's own thought apparent through sound with verbs and nouns (206d1–2). The imagery of the first, we recall, implies a Protagorean world of flux and relativism and is the bare minimum one could expect of any speech: nearly everyone is capable of making such a speech (πᾶς ποιεῖν δυνατὸς) (206d7–8). In response, the second and third attempt to escape the vanity of the first by sufficiently limiting the capacity only to those who know. Both fail, however. The second understands an account as making one "capable (δυνατὸν), when asked what each thing is, to give back an answer through the elements to him who is asking" (206e6–207a1). It fails because one can go through the elements without knowing them, as when one spells the name ΘΕΑΙΤΗΤΟΣ (Theaetetus) correctly by beginning with ΘΕ (The), while spelling ΘΕΟΔΟΡΟΣ (Theodorus) erroneously by beginning with ΤΕ (Te) (207a2–208b10). The third understanding holds that an account makes one "able to say (τὸ ἔχειν...εἰπεῖν) some sign by which the thing asked about differs from all things" (208c7–8). The third fails because it is redundant, inasmuch as a true opinion on its own, without an account, must already be about the difference of each thing from the rest (209d1–3). Socrates uses the example of the parts of Theaetetus' face, which, if opined with insufficient specificity, could be mistaken for that of Socrates (209b2–c11). In sum, the first lapsed momentarily into Protagorean relativism, the second showed that to enumerate the parts of a thing one must make reference to the whole, and the third could only specify the difference of one whole from another with reference to their parts. That is, it appears that Socrates embeds in his refutation of Theaetetus' third definition of knowledge the very problem Parmenides imparted to him—Socrates—as a youth: how the problem of parts and wholes gives rise to the difficulty of responding to the

Protagorean skeptic. As the examples suggest, Theaetetus now resembles both his teachers, Socrates and Theodorus.

We can state the problem more generally as follows. The mathematician demands of his knowledge an unassailable necessity that appears to make geometry and its closest kin the sole true sciences. Whereas an imperialist mathematician like Young Socrates is inclined to extend this demand to the other sciences, an isolationist mathematician like Theaetetus inclines rather to restricting himself to those studies that readily admit of a mathematical approach. For this reason, Theaetetus finds Protagorean relativism attractive: though it undermines what little knowledge he's acquired, it affirms his more general befuddlement about all that is. Socrates' approach has been to offer Theaetetus such dialectical accomplishments as might serve as evidence of his greater ability. But his approach has relied on the promise that he may eventually deliver out of Theaetetus' birth-pangs of perplexity a bouncing baby truth. Socrates cannot deliver on this promise, however, as his entire life has been guided by the Parmenidean insight that pure unity is beyond man's ken—that human wisdom is a necessarily paltry, impure thing. Theaetetus thus finds himself trapped between a relativism he associates with a lack of manliness and a newly-acquired mathematical imperialism destined to flounder on the Parmenidean problem of the unspeakability of pure unity. Rather than emphasize this problem for Theaetetus, Socrates returns to the youth's definition of knowledge as a true opinion with an account, a definition borrowed from the geometer's toolbox. And there he shows Theaetetus that no matter where he turns—whether to Protagorean relativism or the ontology of method—still the problem of knowing impure unity, of knowing a whole of parts, remains just that: a *problem*. Yet as a problem, it makes intelligible the confounding *experience* of knowledge. And according to that experience, the parts of knowledge are separable and enumerable—these are the sciences Theaetetus listed in his original attempt to answer Socrates' question—while the whole of knowledge remains elusive and definable only relative to what it isn't—it is some one thing beyond perception, some gathering-together or gathering-up with respect to our perceptions. That knowledge is intelligibly many but unintelligibly one is to be expected: if anything known admits of an easy enumeration of parts and an only problematic collection into a whole, then so too knowledge, inasmuch as it is something known, will admit of a similarly easy enumeration and problematic collection. Knowledge must be an instance of itself *qua* problem, if it is itself to be intelligible.

Consequently, in place of the geometer's definition of knowledge, Socrates has given Theaetetus the problem or perplexity (ἀπορία) of knowledge, a version of the Stranger's Parmenidean understanding of being *qua* impasse (ἄπορον εἶδος). Far from being a midwife, then, Socrates has fathered in Theaetetus an offspring that bears a resemblance to both its parents—a perplexity every bit as much Theaetetan as it is Socratic. Socrates is erotic.[19] Chapter One's tragedy of the heroic Socrates' fall before his lifelong enemy Protagoras is thus transformed into the sort of romantic comedy befitting its satyr-faced lovers Socrates and Theaetetus. That the final perplexity is Theaetetus' version of Socrates' version of Parmenides' problem affirms that Socratic conversation or dialectics is rife with apparitions (φαντάσματα). But Socrates has not left Theaetetus with just *any* apparition. Had Socrates wanted to do that, he could have affirmed Theaetetus' third definition and departed—*per impossibile*—to get his indictment. The specific apparition is rather a perplexity arising within Theaetetus' opinions, that is, his standard of geometrical precision and the concomitant demand that knowledge be purified of all ignorance. As a shift away from the apparition of Theaetetus' third definition of knowledge, it

---

[19] Within reason, of course. An important feature of the trilogy is the nearly entire absence of ἔρως from Socrates' and the Stranger's self-characterizations as midwife and hunter/searcher, respectively.

must be something more.[20] Indeed, as a perplexity arising from these opinions that exposes their merely partial truth, such an apparition would emphatically point beyond itself to being, so that it would appear also to have the status of a semblance (εἰκών). That is, a Socratic refutation, in exposing a perceived incoherence in one's opinions, is at once an apparition and a semblance, inasmuch as it is a genuine question about a spurious answer. Perhaps it is for this reason that the Stranger was willing to make do with any speech available, even one of questionable veracity (see *Sophist* 251a1–3, 254c6–8). Like the *Theaetetus* itself, such apparitional speech appears complete in itself, while having manifest omissions (see 143b5–c7). It is a self-conscious beauty.

Socratic refutation thus manages to combine the art of making apparitions that distort the beings (φανταστική) with an art of making semblances that accurately represent them (εἰκαστική), specifically by identifying a genuine perplexity within the distortions of a particular opinion or set of opinions.[21] As Theaetetus understands it, one is perfect in point of knowledge when one has plaited together (συμπλακέντα) the names of the beings into a speech (202a7–c5). But we have seen that this is just a distortion expressing Theaetetus' wish to demonstrate decisively that the beings are as he opines them, to have knowledge conform to the geometer's standard of justified true belief, the model of the Euclidean proof. If, rather, we come across an accurate semblance of the beings in the refutation

---

[20] "The effect of the *Theaetetus* has been to convince Theaetetus that any solution to the problem of knowledge is pseudo-wisdom, but he has been convinced without ever gaining anything but a phantom image of the true problem and by taking Socrates for the sophist. The *Theaetetus* seems to suggest that Theaetetus's ignorance of the true problem and his mistaking Socrates for a sophist are one and the same" (Benardete 2000, 321).

[21] This is, on Benardete's reading, the very challenge Parmenides set before Socrates when he met him in his youth. "Socrates is to learn how to replace the gods with the ideas and incorporate them into an ontological psychology," whose speeches would, as ontology, be εἰκόνες and, as psychology, φαντάσματα (Benardete 2012, 238 with 239–40).

of a distortive apparition, then knowledge, in all its impurity, is to be found in the wakeful unraveling of these speeches in light of the problems in being itself. But what could such Penelopean unraveling be but the diacritical core of statecraft, the private refutation of the statesman's public legislation? Socrates sought out a talented young geometer unwilling to take his talents elsewhere, coaxed him beyond his chosen studies, and challenged him to image his standard of knowledge in speech. Socrates need only become a "midwife" to convince Theaetetus to image his perplexity in speech—indeed, to find such an imaging satisfying as a form of knowing: though they were earlier dissatisfied with having discovered only what knowledge isn't and not what it is (187a1–3), by the end of the dialogue they both find that Theaetetus' advances in terms of his character more than compensate for whatever dissatisfaction they might otherwise have had with the negative results (210a7–d2).[22] Theodorus, of course, missed all that. Nevertheless, by satisfying this young scientist with an understanding of his ignorance, Socrates shows

---

[22] What differentiates the two is not so much the result—a woven-together definition preserves something of the question it purports to answer—as it is the disposition toward that definition or the activity guiding its proposal and the subsequent treatment of that proposal, what Socrates had earlier referred to as learning and forgetting (188a2–4). In the *Hippias Major*, Socrates splits himself in two, with one version of him providing Hippias' definitions to the other version of him, who in turn refutes the first version and Hippias at once (*Hippias Major* 286c3–287c1). Though the version of Socrates aligned with Hippias gives the same definitions as Hippias himself, still there is a difference between them in Socrates' willingness to take questions seriously (*Hippias Major* 288c9–d6, 291a3–b2), to accept that his errors have humbled him from any pretense as a knower (*Hippias Major* 286e5–287a1, 287e2–288a5, 289d6–290a2, 291d6–292a7), and to acknowledge that reality is more complex than the simplicity of Hippias' proposals permits (*Hippias Major* 301b2–c3, 304a4–b6). Of course, the actual situation is more complex, as the refutative version of Socrates eventually offers suggestions of his own (*Hippias Major* 293c8–d4). Hippias' lack of humility prevents him from offering new answers that emerge during the conversation (see *Hippias Major* 290c3–d6 with 293d1–e7; also, 295a1–6, 297d10–e2).

how he combines the sophist's refutations with the statesman's nurturing into a single activity called philosophy. In this way, the *Theaetetus* serves as the missing fourth dialogue, the *Philosopher*.

IV.

The above suffices to show how the *Theaetetus* not only introduces the trilogy but finishes it off as its missing fourth. It is fitting, therefore, to conclude this chapter and the book as a whole by returning to the question that the *Philosopher* was to answer, namely, whether the sophist, statesman, and philosopher are one, two, or three (*Sophist* 216d3–217a9). Thereafter we will be in a position to discern the relevance of Plato's defense of Socrates, against the indictment that political philosophy is unscientific, for the crisis induced by the modern scientific project (see Overture).

The sophist and philosopher both practice an art of apparition making (φανταστική), though the manner of their apparition-making differs in an essential respect, namely, in that the philosopher manages to combine the sophist's art of apparition-making with an art of semblance-making (εἰκαστική). Though both sophist and philosopher may confound, the philosopher alone induces a wonder that points beyond himself and to what is. Put differently, the sophist tends to silence his interlocutor, while the philosopher finds a conversation hidden within an opinion; for this reason, Socrates consistently characterized his final two versions of Theaetetus' last definition as latently dialectical (*Theaetetus* 206e6–207a1, 208c7–8).[23] It is this tendency toward raising problems that keeps the philosopher, and his suitably disposed interlocuter, attuned to the fundamental elusiveness of the whole and away from the mere shadows in which the sophist dwells. Among those shadows dwells also the statesman, inasmuch as the work of legislation also deals in distortive apparitions. The Stranger characterized as a host of sophists the myriad regimes that the statesman's legislation, both written

---

[23] See Benardete 2000, 319.

and unwritten, reflects. But for this same reason, the laws are essentially incapable of addressing all particular circumstances. The scientific statesman must therefore take occasional recourse to extralegal measures if he is to further the common good. Though the sophist imitates such lawlessness (ἀνομία), specifically in the form of the tyrant, the statesman's lawlessness, his unraveling of the laws, is done rather in light of the great problems or perplexities in being. In this respect, the statesman practices privately a version of the philosopher's public refutations.

The statesman and philosopher, then, share in something the sophist does not, a private inquiry that scrutinizes one's opinions in light of the perplexities in being itself. But as the *Theaetetus* has shown us, the philosopher's semblance-making is identical to his apparition-making, for a perplexity necessarily emerges in a particular set of opinions: its essence is inseparable from its appearance. The statesman and philosopher's respective apparitions thus differ, inasmuch as the statesman's take the form of opinions or laws, while the philosopher's take the form of a perplexity. That is, the apparitions that the statesman makes promise to provide, while the philosopher's leave one without recourse or resource. In a strange way, then, the philosopher's private and public personae are identical. Statesman and philosopher are one in their use of a private art of semblance-making that necessarily contains within it an aporetic art of apparition-making; they are two, however, in that the statesman conceals his use of the philosopher's combination of the two beneath a legislative art of apparition-making. The statesman is the philosopher clothed in the sophist's noblest apparel. Viewed in light of the philosopher, then, the sophist emerges as a mere shade and the statesman as having being only by virtue of overlapping with the philosopher. Plato's Socrates is the unit by which the sophist and statesman must be measured and thus exposed as lacking the integrity political life lends them.[24] But what gives Socrates his unity is meager in comparison to the reputations of the sophist and statesman. It is nothing more than his knowledge of ignorance, his attending to the all-too-real perplexities that surround us. Yet, as the *Statesman* has shown us, such knowledge of ignorance nevertheless lies at the core of political life. The city's preeminent knowers are but minor players in this triumvirate of ignorants, whose arrangement reflects faintly the perplexity that pervades the whole.

That perplexity has consistently turned out to be the question of the good life, of man's place in the world, the opacity of which serves as Plato's defense of and grounds for Socratic political philosophy. Conversely, the scientist, or rather the imperialist scientist, wishes to grasp the world with mathematical precision, as predictable as a machine. This ambitious wish, reflected in the disposition of Young Socrates, was advanced as a political project in early modernity. The early modern philosophers presented a visionary solution to the political problem of how we are to live together. Yet that solution required narrowing our understanding of human nature to the lowest, material needs, making us into frightened lovers of gain concerned primarily with our bodies and the bodies of the things around us. Those not content with such goods, the ambitious, were consoled with praise for scientific innovation, so that the souls of the courageous and the moderate could be woven together into an

---

[24] Klein concludes that they are two, collapsing the statesman's activity with that of the philosopher, while referring back to his discussion of the middle of the dialogue (Klein 1977, 200 with 172–77). The crucial insight appears to be that scientific statecraft "cannot be said to be confined to the ruling of men in city-states. It has to encompass the ability to argue about the most comprehensive entities in order to do what the Philosopher does" (Klein 1977, 200). Yet between these passages, Klein follows the Stranger through his separation of the royal art from the sophistic statesmen. According to Klein, then, the three men are two, with the statesman falling in either with the sophist or the philosopher. Klein's view differs slightly from my own, for reasons stated above.

apparently seamless political community. Such were our models, the examples (παραδείγματα) we were to emulate. And emulate we did, until the nagging question of happiness, of the good life, popped up again at this beautiful vision's seams, until then barely visible, and exposed that vision for just what it was, but a vision—in the Stranger's terms, what appeared to resemble the beautiful (τὸ φαινόμενον...ἐοικέναι τῷ καλῷ) because we did not view it from a beautiful position (οὐκ ἐκ καλοῦ) (*Sophist* 236b4–5). In its oversimplification of human happiness, this vision did not overcome but rather begged the question of the good in truth.

We do well to reacquaint ourselves today with what Socrates knew millennia ago, that the grounds of our political and practical life are necessarily specious but never wholly arbitrary. All education involves following the models enshrined in law and imaging them in our own conduct. Such models are necessarily partial, and the world inevitably exposes that partiality by presenting unforeseen problems. Every prudent lawgiver and statesman has known this and sought quietly and delicately to adjust their people's laws and ways so as to preserve or even improve their communities. Socrates, however, understood that the failure to sustain a political community indefinitely is not just a problem of practical politics. It rather provides a fundamental insight into the nature of the whole, namely, its recalcitrance to formalization, to comprehension under the strictures of predictability and precision. Plato introduces the scientifically minded to this recalcitrance by showing his reader that the classes or species that inform our deductions are necessarily imaged on models or examples from experience. Everything said is a spoken image, and as an image its accuracy to what is imaged is inherently suspect. It is for this reason that modern natural science is progressive, as new phenomena expose prior theories as merely partial. We respond to such developments by adapting our theories to the new evidence, but rarely do we reflect on this tendency of the world to expose as a partial truth our apparently precise and complete knowledge of a thing. Still more rarely do we make such reflection the core of our scientific pursuits. But isn't this tendency of the world, its recalcitrance to formalization, every bit as much a part of the world as is its susceptibility to formalization? And if so, mustn't this recalcitrance be made central to the scientist's understanding of reality, lest he fail before his own tribunal?

Plato's response to this scientific dilemma is rather to make such reflection thematic to science, that is, to subsume science within political philosophy. Just as we never develop a simply accurate semblance of the beings, save through the refutation of a distortive apparition, so too do we never approach philosophy in itself but always from the outside. As we had occasion to suggest in the Overture, Socrates is always split between poet and character, a feature of his so-called irony. We can now state more precisely that Socrates the character—the particular apparition he adopts in this or that dialogue—is a projection of Socrates the poet, who constructs this image with one eye toward his interlocutor and the other eye toward the deeper problem he detects lurking in that interlocutor's understanding of things and in his own, at once.[25] Socrates "is" a midwife only insofar as he comes into contact with Theaetetus, and he "is" the Achillean gadfly—a self-ennobling pest—only insofar as he must defend his activity before Athens at large. Such images of himself are necessary to draw his interlocutors in, but they are also borne of his awareness of the inextricability of the analogical from the logical. This same awareness guided the Stranger in departing from his method of division, which viewed the true in abstraction from the good, by employing a myth, which is governed not by the true but by the beautiful. There is no demonstration (ἀπόδειξις) free of models and examples (παραδείγματα), for all scientific distinctions are based on the necessarily partial evidence of experience. Faced with this problem, there is every temptation to dismiss the true, as Protagoras did, and so restrict wisdom or expertise (σοφία) to the good as relative, or to dismiss the good as distortive, as the Stranger offered, and restrict science to the true alone.

---

[25] See Priou 2019, 254–55, 266–67.

Only Socrates explicitly sought both, the good in truth, while acknowledging that the beautiful is the intractably problematic point of entry to our discernment of that good. In so doing, he redeemed not only his own dabbling in sophistry but also his student Plato's use of poetry. But in neither Socratic sophistry nor Platonic poetry is the beautiful used merely as embellishment or adornment; rather, both engage in the conscious, rational manipulation of the beautiful for the arousal of another's curiosity.

Plato thus guides us to see how essential the experience of the beautiful or noble (τὸ καλόν) is to the fundamental question of political philosophy, the question of the good life. It is an inevitable, human tendency to become attracted to a *vision* of the good life, to take it as a model to be imaged in one's conduct. A rarer, but still all-too-human tendency is to sense that this vision is, upon closer inspection, not wholly adequate to the question of the good life, that it falls short of the good in truth. This experience, so fundamental to Socratic political philosophy but also simply to living well, is available to us only by virtue of our attraction to the beautiful. The beautiful, we recall, has a paradoxical duality. On the one hand, it can captivate us into believing that it *is* the good in truth, by whose guidance we ought to live; on the other, it can direct us to the larger *question* of the human good. It appears complete in itself, while nevertheless pointing beyond itself to what it claims to be. In this sense, the beautiful or noble (τὸ καλόν) is the point of entry to considering the good in truth, which consequently and necessarily recedes from view. It is some such thought concerning the elusiveness of man's place in the whole, and therefore of the whole itself, that inclined the Stranger to understand being as impassable (ἄπορον εἶδος), to see a nagging question behind any assumed end (τέλος) governing the organization of a whole.[26] Faced with such a limitless understanding of philosophy, the isolationist Theaetetus retreated into

---

[26] Cropsey rightly draws a connection between the question of intelligibility and Theaetetus' pet concerns: "The irrational and the incomprehensible

mathematics while the imperialist Young Socrates advanced into the epistemic homogeneity demanded by methodology. Combining Young Socrates' name with Theaetetus' looks, and Theaetetus' moderation with Young Socrates' courage, Socrates comes to embody the nagging question at the center of any whole, including *the* whole.

For this reason, it seems, Socrates' defense before the Athenian jury, his attempted demonstration (*Apology of Socrates* 20d2–4: πειράσομαι ἀποδεῖξαι) of his innocence, came in the form of showing how the god made him an example or model of human wisdom (ἐμὲ παράδειγμα ποιούμενος) (*Apology of Socrates* 23a7–b4). Nevertheless, Socrates had to portray himself as directed to this wisdom by the god, however beyond belief that portrayal and however avoidant of the source of his wisdom his defense as a whole may have been (see Section I). The Athenian jury, at least, was inclined to respond to the elusiveness of the whole not through the unexamined life Socrates embodied but through pious obedience to the laws—to agree with Meletus that it is not Socrates but the laws and those educated by the laws that redound to the benefit of their fellow citizens (*Apology of Socrates* 24d9–e8). It is no accident that Plato interrupts our sequence—*Theaetetus, Sophist, Statesman,* and "*Theaetetus*" again but as the missing *Philosopher*—with two dialogues on piety and justice, the *Euthyphro* and the *Apology of Socrates*. Plato's dialogues on science bring such proud, scientific types as are characterized therein and as are inevitably attracted thereto—such scientifically minded individuals as might have made it this far—down from the heavens and into the cities, to science's natural context and so its proper object. Socrates' proclamations as to his barrenness, his inability to escape his ignorance, and his paltriness in speeches are not indictments of but testaments to his manner of inquiry as properly scientific. His is a science cognizant of the elusiveness of

---

in mathematics…are the sign that the whole is intractable in itself" (Cropsey 1995, 34; see, also, 29).

the whole and how that makes precarious science's place in the whole.

The power of Socrates as a model or example—rather, as an exemplar—lies in how the publicity of his activity, political philosophy, evinced this connection between the mundane and the profound, the surface and the depth, the simple and the sophisticated, all through the exposure of the pervasiveness of human ignorance. This fundamental ignorance is threatening to all would-be knowers, based as it is on the inherent difficulty of putting the whole together out of its parts, and the questions that difficulty inevitably raises. But the ignorance that exposes these "knowers" as non-entities rather affirms Socrates' being. Of course, the dark and difficult upshot of all this is that Socratic political philosophy, primary as it might be to the essence of the human, is so elusive as to seem non-existent, or at least to seem other than it is. It is on account of the ignorance of others (διὰ τὴν τῶν ἄλλων ἄγνοιαν), Socrates confessed, that the philosopher appears to be of all sorts (παντοῖοι) and not as he is (*Sophist* 216c4–7). In the case of Socrates, this ignorance, even among "knowers" like Theodorus, led to the conclusion that Socrates is a criminal. And while we today may not sentence the philosopher to death, our most renowned "knowers" with glee pronounce philosophy dead and so issue a death-sentence of their own. This pronouncement is but a contemporary reminder of the old and grim lesson, concerning the problem of political philosophy, imparted by Athens' judgment against Socrates, *to* Socrates. As he sat in prison, patiently and painstakingly recounting his conversation with Theaetetus to Euclides, Socrates knew all-too-well that knowledge of ignorance, the principle that explains the city, can never rule within it. The city rewards him, who is most of all, with non-being.

BIBLIOGRAPHY

Aristotle. *Metaphysics.* C. D. C. Reeve, trans. Indianapolis: Hackett Publishing, 2016.

———. *Nicomachean Ethics.* Robert C. Bartlett and Susan D. Collins, trans. Chicago: University of Chicago Press, 2011.

———. *Ethica Nicomachea.* Ingram Bywater, ed. Oxford: Oxford University Press, 1894.

———. *Metaphysica.* Werner Jaeger, ed. Oxford: Oxford University Press, 1957.

Ayer, A. J. *The Problem of Knowledge.* London: Macmillan, 1956.

Bacon, Francis. *The Advancement of Learning.* G. W. Kitchin, ed. Philadelphia: Paul Dry Books, 2001.

———. *New Atlantis and The Great Instauration.* Jerry Weinberger, ed. Second Edition. New York: Wiley Blackwell, 2017.

Bartlett, Robert C. *Sophistry and Political Philosophy: Protagoras' Challenge to Socrates.* Chicago: University of Chicago Press, 2016.

———. "On Law and the Science of Politics in Plato's *Statesman*." In *Plato's* Statesman*: Dialectic, Myth, and Politics*, edited by John Sallis, 237–49. Albany: State University of New York Press, 2017.

Bartlett, Robert C. and Collins, Susan D. (trans.). 2011. *Aristotle's Nicomachean Ethics.* Chicago: University of Chicago Press.

Benardete, Seth. *The Being of the Beautiful: Plato's* Theaetetus, Sophist, *and* Statesman. Chicago: University of Chicago Press, 1984.

———. *Socrates' Second Sailing: On Plato's Republic.* Chicago: University of Chicago Press, 1989.

———. *The Argument of the Action.* Chicago: University of Chicago Press, 2000.

———. *Plato's Symposium.* Chicago: University of Chicago Press, 2001.

———. *The Archaeology of the Soul*. Chicago: University of Chicago Press, 2012.

———. "Two Paradigms." In *The Eccentric Core: The Thought of Seth Benardete*, edited by Ronna Burger and Patrick Goodin, 303–9. South Bend, IN: St. Augustine's Press, 2018.

Benson, Hugh. "The Dissolution of the Problem of the Elenchus." *Oxford Studies in Ancient Philosophy* 13, (1995): 45–112.

Berman, Robert. "The Socratic Principle and the Problem of Punishment." In *The Eccentric Core: The Thought of Seth Benardete*, edited by Ronna Burger and Patrick Goodin, 125–42. South Bend, IN: St. Augustine's Press, 2018.

Blitz, Mark. *Plato's Political Philosophy*. Baltimore: Johns Hopkins University Press, 2010.

Bloom, Allan. "The Ladder of Love." In *Plato's Symposium*, edited by Seth Benardete, 55–178. Chicago: University of Chicago Press, 2001.

Bolotin, David. "The *Theaetetus* and the Possibility of False Opinion." *Interpretation: A Journal of Political Philosophy* 15 (1987): 179–93.

Burger, Ronna. "Socratic εἰρωνεία." *Interpretation: A Journal of Political Philosophy* 13 (1985): 143–50.

———. *Encounters & Reflections: Conversations with Seth Benardete*. Chicago: University of Chicago Press, 2002.

Burger, Ronna and Goodin, Patrick. *The Eccentric Core: The Thought of Seth Benardete*. South Bend, IN: St. Augustine's Press, 2018.

Burnyeat, Myles. *The Theaetetus of Plato*. Indianapolis, IN: Hackett, 1990.

Chisholm, Roderick M. *Perceiving: A Philosophical Study*. Ithaca: Cornell University Press, 1957.

Cornford, Francis M. *Plato's Theory of Knowledge*. Indianapolis: Liberal Arts Press, 1957.

Coxon, A. H. *The Fragments of Parmenides*. Revised and expanded by Richard McKirahan. Las Vegas: Parmenides Publishing, 2009.

Cropsey, Joseph. *Plato's World: Man's Place in the Cosmos*. Chicago: University of Chicago Press, 1995.

Cunliffe, Richard John. *A Lexicon of the Homeric Dialect*. Norman, OK: The University of Oklahoma Press, 1963.

Daube, David. *The Sudden in the Scriptures*. Leiden: Brill, 1964.

Davis, Michael. "On the Being of *The Being of the Beautiful*." In *The Eccentric Core: The Thought of Seth Benardete*, edited by Ronna Burger and Patrick Goodin, 219–31. South Bend, IN: St. Augustine's Press, 2018a.

———. "Seth Benardete's Second Sailing: On the Spirit of Ideas." In *The Eccentric Core: The Thought of Seth Benardete*, edited by Ronna Burger and Patrick Goodin, 101–24. South Bend, IN: St. Augustine's Press, 2018b.

Dinan, Matthew. "On Wolves and Dogs: The Eleatic Stranger's Socratic Turn in the *Sophist*" in Dustin and Schaeffer 2013, 115–39.

Dorter, Kenneth. *Form and Good in Plato's Eleatic Dialogues*. Berkeley: University of California Press, 1994.

Descartes, René. *Meditations on First Philosophy*. Translated by Donald A. Cress. Indianapolis: Hackett Publishing, 1993.

———. *Discourse on the Method*. Richard Kennington, trans, and Pamela Kraus and Frank Hunt, eds. Newburyport: Focus Publishing, 2007.

Dustin, Christopher and Schaeffer, Denise, eds. *Socratic Philosophy and Its Others*. Lanham: Lexington Books, 2013.

Fine, Gail, ed. *Plato I: Metaphysics and Epistemology*. Oxford: Oxford University Press, 1999.

Frede, Michael. "Plato's *Sophist* on False Statements." In *The Cambridge Companion to Plato*, edited by Richard Kraut, 397–424. Cambridge: Cambridge University Press, 1992.

Gettier, Edmund. "Is Justified True Belief Knowledge?" *Analysis* 23 (1963): 121–23.

Gill, Mary Louise. *Philosophos: Plato's Missing Dialogue*. Oxford: Oxford University Press, 2012.

Gómez-Lobo, Alfonso. "Plato's Description of Dialectic in the *Sophist* 253d1–e2." *Phronesis* 22 (1977): 29–47.

Hawking, Stephen and Leonard Mlodinow. *The Grand Design.* New York: Bantam Books, 2010.

Hawking, Stephen and Roger Penrose. *The Nature of Space and Time.* Princeton: Princeton University Press, 1996.

Hopkins, Burt C. "The Philosophers in Plato's Trilogy." In *Plato's Statesman: Dialectic, Myth, and Politics*, edited by John Sallis, 269–83. Albany: State University of New York Press, 2017.

Howland, Jacob. *The Paradox of Political Philosophy.* Lanham: Rowman & Littlefield, 1998.

Hyland, Drew. "Strange Encounters: Theaetetus, Theodorus, Socrates, and the Eleatic Stranger." *Proceedings of the Boston Area Colloquium in Ancient Philosophy* 30 (2015): 103–21.

———. "Stranger than the Stranger: *Axiothea*." In *Plato's* Statesman*: Dialectic, Myth, and Politics*, edited by John Sallis, 223–35. Albany: State University of New York Press, 2017.

Klein, Jacob. *A Commentary on Plato's* Meno. Chapel Hill: University of North Carolina Press, 1965.

———. *Plato's Trilogy:* Theaetetus, *the* Sophist, *and the* Statesman. Chicago: University of Chicago Press, 1977.

Knorr, Wilbur Richard. *The Evolution of the Euclidean Elements: A Study of the Theory of Incommensurable Magnitudes and Its Significance for Early Greek Geometry.* Dordrecht: D. Reidel, 1975.

Kraut, Richard, ed. *The Cambridge Companion to Plato.* Cambridge: Cambridge University Press, 1992.

Kurke, Leslie. "Inventing the 'Hetaira': Sex, Politics, and Discursive Conflict in Archaic Greece." *Classical Antiquity* 16 (1997): 106–50.

Leibowitz, David. *The Ironic Defense of Socrates: Plato's* Apology. Cambridge: Cambridge University Press, 2010.

Lesher, J. H. "Perceiving and Knowing in the *Iliad* and *Odyssey*." *Phronesis* (1981): 26, 2–24.

———. "The Emergence of Philosophical Interest in Cognition." *Oxford Studies in Ancient Philosophy* 12 (1994): 1–34.

Liddell, Henry George, Robert Scott, Henry Stuart Jones, and Roderick McKenzie. *A Greek-English Lexicon*. 9th ed. Oxford: Oxford University Press, 1996.

Locke, John. *Two Treatises of Government*. Peter Laslett, ed. Cambridge: Cambridge University Press, 1988.

———. *Political Writings*. David Wootton, ed. Indianapolis: Hackett Publishing, 1993.

Machiavelli, Niccolò. *The Prince*. Harvey C. Mansfield, trans. Second Edition. Chicago: University of Chicago Press, 1998.

Marcovich, Miroslav. *Heraclitus: Greek Text with a Short Commentary*. Merida: Los Andes University Press, 1967.

Miller, Mitchell. *The Philosopher in Plato's Statesman*. Las Vegas: Parmenides Publishing, 2004.

———. "What the Dialectician Discerns: A reading of *Sophist* 253d–e." *Ancient Philosophy* 36 (2016): 321–52.

Nails, Debra. *The People of Plato*. Indianapolis: Hackett, 2002.

Notomi, Noburu. *The Unity of Plato's Sophist*. Cambridge: Cambridge University Press, 1999.

———. "Reconsidering the Relations between the Statesman, the Philosopher, and the Sophist." In *Plato's Statesman: Dialectic, Myth, and Politics*, edited by John Sallis, 183–95. Albany: State University of New York Press, 2017.

Owen, G. E. L. "Plato on Not-Being." In *Plato I: Metaphysics and Epistemology*, Gail Fine, ed. Oxford: Oxford University Press, 1999.

Patterson, Richard. *Image and Reality in Plato's Metaphysics*. Indianapolis: Hackett Publishing, 1985.

Penrose, Roger. *The Road to Reality*. New York: Vintage Books, 2004.

Plato. *Opera I*. E. A. Duke, W. F Hicken, W. S. M. Nicoll, D. B. Robinson, and J. C. G. Strachan, eds. Oxford: Oxford University Press, 1995.

———. *Opera II*. John Burnet, ed. Oxford: Oxford University Press, 1903.

———. *Opera III*. John Burnet, ed. Oxford: Oxford University Press, 1903.

———. *Rempublicam*. S. R. Slings, ed. Oxford: Clarendon Press, 2003.

Priou, Alex. 2016. "Irony and Opinion: Plato's *Theaetetus* and the Absent Philosopher." *The International Journal of the Platonic Tradition* 10 (2016): 151–67.

———. "On Two Socratic Questions." *St. John's Review* 58.2 (2017): 77–91.

———. *Becoming Socrates: Political Philosophy in Plato's* Parmenides. Rochester: University of Rochester Press, 2018a.

———. "Parmenides on Reason and Revelation." *Epoché: A Journal for the History of Philosophy* 22.2 (2018b): 177–202.

———. "Plato's *Minos* and the *Euthyphro*." *POLIS: The Journal for Ancient Greek Political Thought* 35 (2018c): 145–63.

———. "Approaching Seth Benardete: On *The Eccentric Core*." *Interpretation: A Journal of Political Philosophy* 45 (2019): 249–67.

Robinson, David. "Textual Notes on Plato's *Sophist*," *The Classical Quarterly* 49 (1999): 139–60.

Rosen, Stanley. *Plato's* Statesman*: The Web of Politics*. New Haven: Yale University Press, 1979.

———. *Plato's* Sophist*: The Drama of Original and Image*. New Haven: Yale University Press, 1983.

Sallis, John, ed. *Plato's* Statesman*: Dialectic, Myth, and Politics*. Albany: State University of New York Press, 2017.

Smyth, Herbert Weir. *A Greek Grammar*. New York: American Book Company, 1920.

Sophocles. *The Theban Plays:* Oedipus the Tyrant, Oedipus at Colonus, Antigone. Peter J. Ahrensdorf and Thomas L. Pangle, trans. Ithaca: Cornell University Press, 2014.

———. *Fabulae*. Lloyd-Jones, Hugh and N. G. Wilson, eds. Oxford: Clarendon Press, 1990.

Speliotis, Evanthia. "Φρόνησις and Law in Plato's *Statesman*," *Ancient Philosophy* 31 (2011): 295–310.

———. "Sophist and Philosopher in Plato's *Sophist*." In *Socratic Philosophy and Its Others*, edited by Christopher Dustin and Denise Schaeffer, 197–215. Lanham, MD: Lexington Books, 2013.

Spinoza, Baruch. *The Letters*. Translated by Samuel Shirley. Indianapolis: Hackett Publishing, 1995.

Stern, Paul. *Knowledge and Politics in Plato's* Theaetetus. Cambridge: Cambridge University Press, 2008.

Strauss, Leo. *Natural Right and History*. Chicago: University of Chicago Press, 1953.

———. *The City and Man*. Chicago: University of Chicago Press, 1964.

———. "Plato." In *History of Political Philosophy*, third edition, edited by Leo Strauss and Joseph Cropsey, 33–89. 1987.

———. *On Plato's Symposium*. Edited by Seth Benardete. Chicago: University of Chicago Press, 2001.

Strauss, Leo and Joseph Cropsey, eds. *History of Political Philosophy*. Third Edition. Chicago: University of Chicago Press, 1987.

Umphrey, Stewart. *The Aristotelian Tradition of Natural Kinds & Its Demise*. Washington, D.C.: Catholic University of America Press, 2018.

Vlastos, Gregory. *Socratic Studies*. Oxford: Oxford University Press, 1994.

von Fritz, Kurt. "ΝΟΟΣ and NOEIN in the Homeric Poems," *Classical Philology* 38 (1943): 79–93.

———. "ΝΟΥΣ, NOEIN, and Their Derivatives in Pre-Socratic Philosophy (Excluding Anaxagoras): Part I. From the Beginnings to Parmenides," *Classical Philology* 40 (1945): 223–42.

Zuckert, Catherine. *Plato's Philosophers: The Coherence of the Dialogues*. Chicago: University of Chicago Press, 2009.

INDEX

Index of Names

Appelbaum, Seth: 97n6

Aristotle: 3n3, 19, 25n4, 70n22, 73, 84, 108, 114, 116n29, 140n4

Benardete, Seth: 9n9, 11n14, 16–17n13, 19n16, 35n13, 43n21, 57n6, 58n8, 66n18, 80n28, 81n29, 90n37, 94n2, 94n4, 110n22, 135n39, 142–43n8, 144n9, 151–52n13, 160n17, 165n20, 165n21, 167n23

Burger, Ronna: viii, 132

Davis, Michael: 94n4, 116n29, 134n37

Descartes, René: 1n1, 2n3, 4n4, 4n5, 4–5n5, 5n6, 46n24, 98

Gill, Mary Louise: 14n11, 60n10, 65–66n16

God: 2n2, 5n6, 11, 40–41, 75n24, 100n9, 105–7, 109n20, 124, 133n36, 138, 173–74

Grewal, Gwenda-lin: 134n38

Heidegger, Martin: 7

Heraclitus: 9n9, 47, 146, 151, 151–52n13

Herodotus: 99, 100, 159

Hippias: 166n22

Homer: 15, 15n12, 16, 16–17n13, 25, 140n4, 146, 152

Howland, Jacob: 14n11, 16n13, 18n15, 54n2, 56n5, 63n13, 66n17, 68–69n20, 70n22, 73n23, 90n37, 99n7, 104n14, 107n16, 107n17, 108n19, 126n33, 141n7

Klein, Jacob: 42n20, 110n21, 134n37, 169n40

Lincoln, Abraham: 68

Nietzsche, Friedrich: 7–8

Oedipus: 15, 100n9, 109n20

Parmenides: viii, 9n9, 10, 13n12, 13n13, 25, 32, 35, 35n13, 39–41, 41n19, 48–49, 51, 55, 58, 70n22, 72, 73, 74–75, 75n24, 76, 76n25, 77, 80, 83, 85, 87, 90, 146, 151, 160–64, 165n21

Penelope: 135, 166

Plato: 3, 7, 13–15, 18–19, 23, 39, 54–55n4, 81n29, 119, 126n33, 131, 132–34, 167, 168–73

Stern, Paul: 17n14, 19n17, 42n20, 133n36, 151–52n13, 159n16

Strauss, Leo: 19n17, 31n10, 66n18, 99n7, 138n2

Zuckert, Catherine: 16n13, 54n3, 56n5, 133n36, 134n38, 140n5, 145n10, 151n12, 160n18

Index of Ideas

analogical vs. logical: 35–38, 43, 51, 55, 59, 86–89, 90, 91, 98, 110–11, 131–32, 153–56, 171

didactic parricide/patricide: 72–75, 87, 90, 101, 110n22, 141, 149, 152, 159

dilemma of intelligibility: 45–46, 157–58

epistemic heterogeneity and homogeneity: 94–95, 98, 100, 118, 173

essential resourcelessness (or impassable species/essential perplexity): 69–71, 74, 83–84, 87, 89, 105–8, 110, 113, 118, 123, 144, 155, 157, 164, 172

God: 10, 24, 38, 36, 43, 53–54, 62, 64–65, 79, 81–83, 87, 98, 105–7, 108n19, 124, 133n36, 138, 148, 165n21, 173–74

mathematicians, imperialist vs. isolationist: 4–5n5, 22, 25, 50, 97–98, 156, 163–64, 169, 172–73

ontology of method: 46, 112, 118, 132, 161–62, 163

paltriness: 11, 37, 41, 53, 54n2, 61, 90n7, 163, 173

pregnancy: 18, 49, 91, 134n38, 143–44

problem of Socrates: 56–59, 66, 69, 71, 78, 90–92, 93–94, 94n3, 119, 167–74

scientific pride: 53, 98–103, 108n19, 109, 111, 118–19, 173 (*contra* 2n2)

second sailing: 16n13, 93, 128

triumvirate of ignorance: 18, 169

the true and the good: 1–8, 9–10, 19, 29–33, 40, 55–56, 66, 81, 91, 103–4, 111, 113, 116, 117, 124, 131, 134, 169–73